# 1001
# Gruesome
# FACTS

# 1001 Gruesome FACTS

The gross, the ghoulish and the ghastly

Helen Otway

**Capella**

This edition published in 2007 by Arcturus Publishing Limited
26/27 Bickels Yard, 151–153 Bermondsey Street,
London SE1 3HA

ISBN: 978-1-84193-732-8

Editors: Kate Overy and Fiona Tulloch

Printed in China

# CONTENTS

# 1001 Gruesome Facts

## Are you ready?

Are you really ready to plumb the depths of gruesomeness...
and beyond? If little things like mucus and blood gross you out,
then read no further. As well as cups of mucus and oodles of
blood, you'll come across a whole host of things you didn't
know about. Who'd have thought that our bodies and the food
we eat could be so disgusting? But animals and the world we
live in are even worse!

Some of us are born gruesome, and others have gruesomeness
thrust upon them. People have been doing the most horrible
things to others since time began; the further back in history you
go, the more gruesome everyday life gets. A popular way for the
Romans to entertain themselves, for example, was to watch men
killing each other. They would pop along to the local death-fest the
way you would go to the cinema...and they didn't even have to
pay to get in!

# Gruesome Gladiators

(Free extras, not part of your 1001 facts!)

If you lived in Roman times, gruesome events you might have seen in your free time included:

*Public executions, where you could settle down, get comfy with a snack and watch a few people being killed in imaginative ways by the state.*

*Chariot races, with the highlight being a chariot pile-up that killed the drivers and the horses! (The life expectancy of a charioteer was very low.)*

*Gladiatorial combat with special guests — wild animals! Stick a young man in an arena with a hungry lion or tiger and see what happens. Excellent fun.*

# Over to you

If you make it to the end of this book without keeling over, well done! Reward yourself by writing down your own gruesome fact to reach the 1001 target. It could be something that happened to you, like seeing your brother eat his earwax, or something that was on TV, like the man who had a snake living in his gut for years without realising why he always felt so hungry.

**Are you sure you're ready?**
**Then dive right in...**

# Don't even think about it!

Okay, so you might want to eat beetroot to see if your urine really does go pink. You might even be tempted to try pig's organ soup next time you're in Singapore – it's good enough for the locals, after all. What you absolutely shouldn't do is try to recreate any of the gruesome stuff in this book yourself. Leave the unpleasant tricks like eating stinging nettles and bathing in cockroaches to the people who have practised their gruesome feats for years and understand the dangers. Take pleasure in knowing that it isn't you…

Florida woman Gayle Grinds was so obese that after spending six years on her couch, her skin became fused to the upholstery.

Nose mucus is normally clear. But if you have a bacterial infection it turns yellow, or even green!

Your appendix looks like a worm dangling from your intestine... and you don't even need it for anything!

Even though your gastric juices are highly acidic, they cannot digest chewing gum. A small piece of gum will pass right through the digestive system, but larger amounts can cause a serious blockage.

There are 250,000 sweat glands in your feet, all working away to make sure your socks smell really cheesy!

If an astronaut burps, it is a sick burp; the lack of gravity means any food is floating about at the top of the stomach!

Your nose produces a cup of mucus each day. Would you like a biscuit with that?

Early x-rays caused nasty side effects such as skin burns, swelling and hair loss.

Spanish artist Salvador Dalí used to study his stools and make notes on their colour and consistency.

The skin you can see on your body is dead! New cells are growing underneath to give you a new layer of skin every 30 days.

*Quinsy*, a complication of tonsillitis, is a putrid abscess in the throat. The sufferer will drool rather than endure the agony of swallowing their saliva.

Australian Graham Barker has been collecting his own belly button fluff every day since 1984 and keeps it in storage jars.

The condition of excessive body hair is called *hypertrichosis*, or Werewolf Syndrome.

Women of the Himalayan Apatani tribe used to enlarge their nostrils with circular, 2.5 centimetres (1 inch) wide nose plugs.

When you crack your knuckles, the noise comes from gas bubbles popping in the liquid around your joints.

A carbuncle is a large abscess on the skin that oozes pus from one or two holes.

Native American man Dennis Avner, otherwise known as Stalking Cat, has gone to great lengths to be tigrine: he has stripes tattooed on his body, his ears have been surgically elongated and he inserts synthetic whiskers into facial piercings.

**Devoted Hindus attending the Malaysian Thaipusam festival stick skewers through their skin as part of the celebrations.**

Each year, 6,500 people are taken to British hospitals after being injured by a lawnmower. Injuries include the slicing off of a toe or even a finger!

Indian man Vijayakanth can pass a thread through his tear duct and out through his mouth in just 60 seconds.

**Blood whizzes through the main artery in the body, the *aorta*, at 30 centimetres (12 inches) a second. If the aorta is cut, imagine how fast the blood spurts out!**

The first time you get a cold sore, the virus that causes it lurks in your body for the rest of your life.

You've got jelly in your bones! It is called *bone marrow* and it makes your blood cells.

Dutch artist Joanneke Meester had a section of skin surgically removed from her abdomen and used it to make a replica pistol as a comment on rising violence.

Whilst playing for Swiss team Servette, Portuguese football player Paulo Diogo tried to jump over a metal barrier during a goal celebration. His wedding ring got caught and he lost the top half of his finger. He even got a yellow card for wasting time!

The body uses 16 different chemicals to create a scab.

A person struck by lightning may have red, snaky patterns on their skin afterwards. These are known as *Lichtenberg figures* or *lightning flowers* and are caused by ruptured blood capillaries.

After being removed from the body, the lungs can survive longer than any other organ.

The *cornea* (the surface of your eye) is the only part of your body that has no blood supply. It is still not a good idea to cut it, though.

You have bones in your body that are not attached to any other bone. These 'floating' bones are your triangular kneecaps and the horseshoe-shaped *hyoid* in your neck.

Bits of dried earwax come loose and fall out when you chew, yawn or swallow!

90 per cent of the hairs on your head are growing at any point during the day. The other 10 per cent are just having a rest!

The sound of a burp is caused by the vibration of the *cardia* (where your stomach and oesophagus meet) when gas from your stomach whizzes through it. More gas means a louder burp.

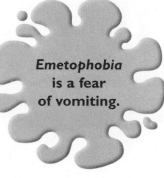

*Emetophobia* is a fear of vomiting.

The heart pumps blood around your body with enough pressure to squirt it 9 metres (30 feet) away.

*Black hairy tongue* is a dark fungal infection that makes the taste buds swell and give the tongue a furry appearance. Its colour can also be green or brown.

American surgeon William Beaumont researched human digestion by putting pieces of food on string and poking them through an old gunshot wound in an ex-patient's stomach. He pulled out the food at intervals to see the effects of digestion on it.

*Pellagra* is a vitamin deficiency disease caused by lack of protein and vitamin B. In severe cases, it is characterised by 'the four d's': diarrhoea, dermatitis, dementia and death.

Maggots have been used for thousands of years to help clean and heal wounds, as they munch away at dead flesh. Some really greedy maggots eat the other maggots too.

Malaria is caused by parasites in the saliva of mosquitoes that get into the human bloodstream. The parasites multiply in the liver and red blood cells.

The temperature of your farts is around 37 degrees Celsius (98.6 degrees Fahrenheit), the same as your body. They might feel hotter if you've eaten something spicy.

Depending on the infection, pus can be white, yellow, brown or blue. Yes, blue!

A Mexican man made a protest against the discrimination of people with tattoos and piercings by putting hooks through his back and arms, using them to dangle himself from a tree.

Short-sighted people have bigger eyeballs than those who are long-sighted.

Wealthy Texan recluse Howard Hughes was so obsessed with protecting his body from germs that he could not use a spoon unless his staff had first covered the handle in layers of tissue paper and cellophane.

You can hear the blood flowing through your ears if you find a quiet place and cover them tightly.

American multi-millionairess Hetty Green was so stingy that she would not pay for her son to have his broken leg treated. He then got gangrene and had to have the limb amputated.

Someone with *cutaneous anthrax* will have large, black ulcers on their skin.

Stick your tongue out! Those bumps on it are called *papillae* and they contain your taste buds. You were born with 10,000 taste buds but they die with age, so your grandparents may have only 5,000.

The skin is the body's largest organ. If you lay it out and smooth out the wrinkles, it can cover an area of up to 2 square metres (7 square feet).

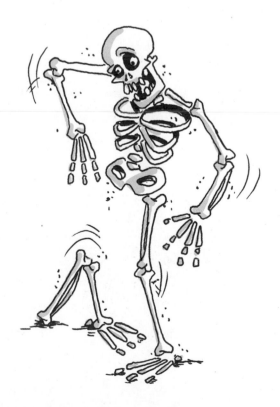

Members of the Native American Mandan tribe used to keep the skulls of their dead and place them in a circle formation near their village.

Bowel obstruction (a blocked bowel) can lead to faecal vomiting, in which faeces are expelled back into the stomach from the colon and up through the mouth.

*Keraunoparalysis* is the temporary paralysis of the legs suffered after being struck by lightning.

In 2004, Uruguayan artist Carlos Capelán exhibited collages made from toenail clippings.

British man Richard Ross inhaled a nail that he was holding between his lips whilst doing DIY in his home. His ribs had to be broken for the subsequent lung surgery to remove it and he spent three weeks in hospital.

Nail files can carry nail fungus, bacteria and viruses.

If the body is fighting an infection, the *lymph nodes* can swell to the size of an orange. We call them 'swollen glands'.

The reclusive Collyer brothers' Harlem house was so full of junk that after Homer Collyer died, police and workmen cleared rubbish for two weeks before they found the body of his brother, Langley.

18th-century footmen, who had to walk closely behind their masters or mistresses, were known colloquially as 'fart-catchers'.

When gas escapes from a dead body, it sounds like the corpse is farting.

One of the first stages of embalming a dead body is called *setting the features*, which includes stitching or gluing the lips together to keep the mouth shut.

An old remedy for warts used to be to rub a piece of raw meat on them and then bury the meat. It was thought that as the meat rotted away, the warts would disappear.

*Tinea cruris* is a fungal infection of the groin area. Sufferers are often sportspeople, so it's commonly known as 'jock itch'!

**Queen Elizabeth I had black teeth. Like most Elizabethans, she was fond of sugary foods but toothbrushes and toothpaste hadn't yet been invented.**

*Obstipation* is severe constipation. If it lasts for days, it can cause bloating, distention and terrible pain.

The deadly poison *strychnine* has a dramatic effect on the body – all the muscles go into spasm, causing convulsions until the back arches and breathing stops. *Rigor mortis* (stiffening) sets in immediately, with the eyes remaining wide open.

Verrucas that grow in clusters are known as *mosaic warts*.

*Clubbing* is a condition that causes the hands to swell up and makes the fingers look like fat sausages. It is caused by liver malfunction.

**After scoring the winning goal against Ecuador in a 2006 World Cup match, England captain David Beckham vomited on the pitch.**

If your breath is a bit stinky in the morning, it's because your saliva glands have slowed down while you were asleep, making your mouth dry. It doesn't take long for them to get back into action again.

Argentinian artist Nicola Constantino has made 100 soaps and two sculptures from her own fat! The fat was removed from her body using liposuction.

A *teratoma*, meaning 'monster tumour', is a rare growth inside the body that can have hair and teeth.

A stool that floats and won't flush away is full of gas.

*Scurvy* used to be a common condition caused by vitamin C deficiency. It would cause spongy gums, loose teeth, purple blotches on the skin and, in extreme cases, death. Anyone for an orange?

**During a severe nosebleed, blood can travel up the sinuses and come out through the eyes.**

Eating lots of beetroot will make your urine pink.

If you ever jump as if you're being electrocuted when drifting off to sleep, you're experiencing a *hypnic jerk*. The brain mistakes pre-sleep relaxation for falling and stiffens the limbs to get the body upright again.

American surfer Bethany Hamilton had her left arm bitten off by a tiger shark but went back to surfing just ten weeks later.

First World War soldiers often suffered from *trench mouth*, in which the gums would swell up and bleed, becoming covered in ulcers. Left untreated, it spread to the cheeks and lips.

Your teeth are soft in the middle! The outside is made of *enamel*, which is the hardest substance in your body. Inside is squidgy stuff called *pulp*, made of nerves, blood vessels and tissue.

Stale urine used to be an ingredient in gunpowder.

Amongst the 103 tonnes of junk removed from the Collyer brothers' house in Harlem were human organs pickled in jars and a horse's jawbone.

A liver with *cirrhosis* is an orangey yellow colour and lumpy.

The deadly *Ebola* virus makes sufferers throw up thick, black vomit.

**Guinea worm disease** is caught from drinking infected water in tropical countries. Between one and two years after infection, a spaghetti-like worm up to 100 centimetres (40 inches) long will pop out of a blister in the foot or leg.

A person who has had an eye removed can suffer from *phantom eye syndrome*; they experience sensations, pain and hallucinations in the missing eye.

Eating potent foods such as chillies and garlic will make your sweat smell stronger.

Tooth decay has been around for thousands of years and in ancient times was believed to have been caused by a 'tooth worm'.

*Major aphthous ulcerations* are mouth ulcers that are more than a centimetre (half an inch) wide. Ouch!

The part of your brain that controls body stuff like vomiting and salivating is called the *medulla.*

Not all dead bodies decompose after burial. If conditions are right, the skin develops a soapy coating called *adipocere* and the body becomes naturally mummified.

One day's worth of your farts is enough to blow up a small balloon.

Squatting is the best position for the body to be in when passing a stool.

Spanish artist Francisco de Goya got lead poisoning from the paints he used and became completely deaf.

If you eat ice cream too quickly, the blood vessels in your head swell up and give you a 'brain freeze' headache. Your nerves send messages to the brain that you're in a cold environment, so the blood vessels swell to warm you up.

Blood is made up of 92 per cent water.

American mountaineer Aron Ralston had to take drastic action when a boulder fell on his arm and pinned him to the ground in Blue John Canyon, Utah. After five days, desperation drove him to amputate the arm with a penknife.

Queen Elizabeth I was so afraid of having one of her rotten teeth extracted that a loyal Archbishop had to have one of his teeth out first to reassure her.

Going up a mountain too quickly will make you vomit! At heights over 2,500 metres (8,000 feet) above sea level, a change in pressure means the body does not get as much oxygen and needs time to acclimatize. If not, altitude sickness will occur.

If you have a cut in your skin, it takes less than 10 seconds for your blood to start clotting to form a scab.

Just like your fingerprints, your tongue print is unique – it's just a bit sloppier!

When Polish man Hubert Hoffman criticized the country's president Lech Kaczynski during a routine police check, he was asked to show more respect. He replied with a loud fart and was promptly arrested!

A 19th-century cure for toothache was to hammer a nail into the tooth and then stick the nail in a tree to transfer the pain.

*Cauliflower ear* is caused by blood clots forming on the ear after being hit or by skin being torn from the ear's cartilage, making ugly lumps and bumps. Boxers often suffer from this, but it's probably best not to point it out if you meet one!

Inventors Michael Zanakis and Philip Femano patented a fart-powered toy rocket in 2005.

Eating asparagus produces a chemical called *methanethiol* that makes urine smell of rotten cabbage.

19th-century English footballer Joe Powell broke his arm so badly during a match that he got tetanus and blood poisoning as a result. His arm was amputated in an attempt to save him, but he died a week later.

The world's most pierced woman, Elaine Davidson, can put her little finger through the hole in her tongue.

Hair cannot turn white with fright, but shock can make pigmented hair suddenly fall out. An older person whose hair is a mixture of colour and grey would then be left with only grey hairs, appearing to turn white overnight.

If your skin did not secrete its naturally antibacterial substances, you would go mouldy!

The rare but fatal brain disease *kuru* is also known as laughing sickness, as its victims go through a stage of bursting into laughter, before they develop ulcerations and eventually die.

NASA aeroplanes used for training astronauts have the nickname 'Vomit Comets', as the weightlessness that passengers experience often makes them throw up.

Characteristics of tetanus are muscle spasms in the jaw and difficulty swallowing, which is why the disease is also known as 'lockjaw'.

Indian man Dharmendra Singh can make cigarette smoke come out of his ears. He can whistle through his nose too!

By the time of her death, Queen Elizabeth I's coronation ring had become embedded in her flesh. The ring had to be sawn off so that it could be passed to the heir to the throne, James VI of Scotland.

Sufferers of *blackwater fever* pass black urine, hence the name.

Brain diseases known as *spongiform encephalopathies* cause the brain to become riddled with holes.

The blood vessels in the conjunctiva (eye membrane) are very fragile. If ruptured, a bright red haemorrhage will spread across the white of the eye.

Italian artist Piero Manzoni filled 90 small tins with his own faeces for a 1961 exhibition. Some of them later exploded!

**Indian painter Shihan Hussaini used over a litre of his blood to paint 56 portraits of politician Jayalalitha for her 56th birthday.**

*Tendons* attach your muscles to your bones and look like rubber bands. Like rubber bands, they can also snap.

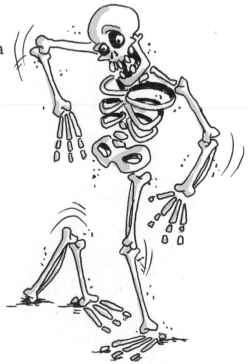

After a car accident in Nottinghamshire, England, a back seat passenger was impaled by a snooker cue that had been in the car's boot. It missed her vital organs and she was released from hospital after only three days.

Turkish construction worker Ilker Yilmaz can snort milk up his nose and squirt it more than 2.5 metres (9 feet)... from his eye!

St. Louis barber Bill Black used the hair clippings swept from his floor to make vests, shirts, ties and even a bikini!

When Canadian man Jim Sulkers died in his bed, his body was not discovered until two years later. The corpse had not decomposed but had become mummified in the hot, dry conditions at the time of his death.

*Helmintophobia* is a fear of being infested with worms. Who wouldn't be scared?

American man Matt Gone was so unhappy with his birthmarks that he has had 94 per cent of his body covered in a checkerboard tattoo.

Three million of your red blood cells die each second! Luckily, your body is replacing them just as quickly – one drop of your blood contains five million red blood cells.

A blister contains lymph and other body fluids. This is what makes them squidgy and tempting to pop!

There are more than 200 species of bacteria living on your skin at any one time. Some are good bacteria that are making themselves useful!

Joseph Merrick, known as 'The Elephant Man', suffered from a rare condition called *Proteus syndrome*, which causes disfiguring skin and bone growths.

Breckenridge carpenter Patrick Lawler suffered eye swelling and toothache after his nail gun backfired and a nail struck his face. When he had an x-ray six days later, it showed a second 10 centimetre (4 inch) nail embedded in his skull!

Some contortionists dislocate their hip or shoulder joints during their displays.

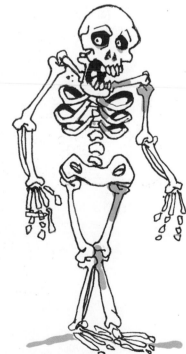

Sylvester the 'Cowboy Mummy' is displayed at Ye Olde Curiosity Shoppe in Seattle. Complete with gunshot wounds, he is preserved in arsenic, commonly used in the 19th century to preserve corpses.

A person who has been struck by lightning may have perforated eardrums, cataracts, burns or permanent brain damage as a result.

*Intestinal myiasis* is a condition where maggots are in a person's stomach. The maggots can be swallowed in infected food and cause cramps, but are eventually digested by gastric juices.

In 2004, Dutch eye surgeons invented eyeball jewellery; the eye membrane is sliced and a decorative shape is inserted. UK and US eye specialists have criticized the practice, since it could cause infection and scarring.

The black dot in the middle of a verruca is its blood supply.

American politician Stan Jones suffered from a condition called *argyria* after taking medicine that contained silver. His skin became permanently grey!

A *nasal polyp* is a fleshy growth in the nostril that can be as big as a grape.

The African tumbu fly lays its eggs in clothes. When the clothes are worn, the eggs hatch and the larvae burrow into the skin, creating boil-like sores for the maggots to grow in.

You had more than 300 bones when you were born, but by the time you're an adult you'll have only 206! Don't worry, you won't lose them – some of your bones will just fuse together.

An average appendix is 10 centimetres (3.94 inches) long. The longest appendix ever removed came from a man in Pakistan: it was 23.5 centimetres (9 inches) long!

When British footballer Darius Vassell had a blood blister under his toenail, he tried to get rid of it… by drilling a hole in the nail himself! His DIY surgery led to an infection and the loss of half his toenail.

*Entropion* is a condition in which the eyelid turns inwards against the eyeball. The skin rubs against the surface of the eyeball and can cause sight loss.

British performance artist Mark McGowan spent two weeks sitting on a London street with his raised arm strapped to a lamppost, draining the blood from his arm and possibly causing muscle damage. He called this anti-war protest *The Withered Arm.*

All your bodily functions stop when you sneeze... even your heartbeat!

*Catgut,* used for stitching cuts, is made from sheep or goat intestines.

Fijian rugby player Jone Tawake decided to have his right ring finger amputated when a dislocated joint became infected.

# Gruesome Food Facts

Napoleon's starving troops were told to eat the flesh of horses that had died on the battlefield. They used a sprinkling of gunpowder as seasoning!

A ripe jackfruit smells of rotten onions.

*Entomophagy* is the habit of eating insects – over 1,200 species of insects are gobbled down all over the world.

Animal fat from cooking meat is a common cause of sewer blockages. Thames Water flushers in central London once had to clear a solid lump of fat blocking 45 metres (150 feet) of sewer.

Two Scottish artists used their own blood to make black pudding (blood sausage). As if animal blood isn't disgusting enough?

African delicacy *mopani* worms are emperor moth caterpillars. They are prepared for frying by nipping off the ends and squeezing out the green guts… just like toothpaste from a tube!

*Giblets* are the heart, liver and gizzard (stomach) of a bird. You can eat them all if you want to!

Talcum powder is sometimes used in foods to prevent caking.

The French dish *oreilles de Christ* (Christ's ears) is made with pieces of deep-fried bacon fat. No ears in 'ere!

Cow's milk that has not been pasteurised can contain nasty bacteria, such as tuberculosis, salmonella, E. coli and diphtheria.

You can get Paralytic Shellfish Poisoning (PSP) from eating shellfish that have fed on toxic algae. Muscular and respiratory paralysis (which is death, basically) can occur within hours of digestion.

The edible white larvae of the New Zealand *Huhu* beetle can be up to 7 centimetres (3 inches) long. They taste like buttered chicken.

Butter and yogurt made from camel's milk are light green.

*Livermush* is a popular product in the southern United States, made from pig's liver, pig's head and cornmeal.

Brendan Brockbank won the World Pie-Eating Contest in Wigan, England, by wolfing down a humungous pie in just 37 seconds!

The *fatass ant* – guess what it looks like – has been a traditional Columbian food for hundreds of years and is often given as a wedding gift. Only the queen ants are edible and harvesting them is a painful business.

Used chewing gum was auctioned online in 2004. Pieces chomped by Britney Spears, Christina Aguilera, Eminem and Jessica Simpson were available to interested bidders.

*Black moss* or *hair moss* is a freshwater algae used in Chinese cooking. In its dried form, it looks like black human hair.

> Apple pips contain a small amount of toxic cyanide, which causes vomiting, seizures and cardiac arrest. Don't panic if you swallow one – you'd need large amounts to be poisoned.

> The Burnt Food Museum in Arlington, Massachusetts, showcases black, charred food. The museum had to close down temporarily… due to fire damage!

Tiny, fiery hot chillies used in Thai cooking are known as *phrik khii nuu* – mouse-dropping chillies.

Charles Darwin was president of The Glutton Club at Cambridge University. He and his friends would meet to taste 'strange flesh', including hawk, bittern and owl.

*Pocari Sweat* is the name of a Japanese soft drink that is grey in colour. Mmmm, tempting!

**The French cheese *Époisses de Bourgogne* is so stinky that it is banned from being taken on public transport in France.**

Lead tastes sweet! Wine was sweetened with toxic lead sugar until the 17th century, giving those who drank it gradual lead poisoning.

**British pensioner Margaret Haste keeps a hot cross bun as a reminder of her aunt, who died in 1899. The 108-year-old heirloom is kept wrapped in tissue inside a box.**

British performance artist Mark McGowan turned himself into an English breakfast for two weeks in 2003. He sat in a bath of baked beans with two chips up his nose and 48 sausages strapped to his head.

**Donkey meat was eaten in Britain until the 1930s.**

US researchers ran trials on a drink containing pig whipworm eggs. They found that the hatched worms eased symptoms of bowel disorders in people taking part.

**Fancy a slice of pig's blood sausage, studded with chunks of pickled pig's tongue? Just ask for *zungenwurst* next time you're in Germany!**

*Kumis* is a Central Asian drink, made from horse's milk that is fermented in horse skin containers until slightly alcoholic.

Korean fermented soya bean paste *(doenjang)* smells of rotten fish.

The *fingered citron or Buddha's hand* is a giant citrus fruit so scary-looking that it has also been named *goblin fingers*. Mould can grow between the yellow 'fingers' but when fresh, the fragrant fruit is used for its zest.

Singaporean *pig's organ soup* is a mixture of pig intestine, stomach, blood cubes and pork slices. There are vegetables in it too, but you probably wouldn't notice those.

A young Wisconsin factory worker became trapped in a chocolate vat for two hours after he waded into it up to his waist to pull out the plug. Nearly death by chocolate!

Raw red kidney beans contain a toxic enzyme called *phytohaemagglutinin*, which causes severe vomiting and diarrhoea. The beans are made safe to eat by hours of soaking and boiling. Tinned ones are fine!

A British chef was bitten by a highly venomous Brazilian wandering spider that had been hiding in bananas in his kitchen. He was quick-thinking enough to photograph the spider on his phone so that he could get the right treatment.

*Anticuchos are South American goat heart or cow heart kebabs. A hearty meal on a stick.*

*Fuqi feipian* is a Chinese dish that translates as 'married couple's lung slices' and is made of thin slices of spiced cow's lung, served cold.

**If you refrigerate bananas, you'll give them chill injury! As tropical fruits, they react badly to cold temperatures by going black and squishy.**

*Mad honey intoxication* is caused by eating honey made from rhododendron nectar. Symptoms include vomiting, excessive salivating and sweating, and tingling around the mouth.

Eye protection is recommended for those sampling the maggot-ridden Sardinian delicacy *casu marzu* cheese. The larvae in it can jump as high as 15 centimetres (6 inches) when disturbed!

The first bubble gum was developed in 1906 and was a failure. Called *Blibber-Blubber*, it had a Play-Doh consistency and produced sticky, wet bubbles.

**Filipino 'chocolate pudding' is in fact, a dark brown stew of pig's organs in a spicy pig's blood gravy.**

**The red food colouring carmine (€120) is made from crushed cochineal insects.**

An outbreak of the disease *salmonella* in Britain during the summer of 2005 was traced to lettuces imported from drought-hit southern Spain. Desperate farmers had used their household sewage to water crops.

Dead insects go off quickly so should be eaten alive or immediately after being killed. Hopping insects need to be chilled or frozen before cooking so they don't jump out of the pan!

Japanese *basashi* vanilla ice cream is made with chunks of raw horseflesh. If you don't fancy that, there's always *yagi no aisu:* goat's milk and goat's meat ice cream.

*Oiseaux sans títes* (headless birds) is a Belgian dish of sausage meat wrapped in veal slices.

Comedy actor Steve-O vomited after snorting super-hot Japanese *wasabi* in a stunt for *Jackass: The Movie*.

A bag of flour may be infested with tiny beetles called *weevils* that can spread the deadly E. Coli bacteria. They also like hiding in packets of cereal. You have been warned!

British woman Jo Carter ate 10.3 metres (34 feet) of raw stinging nettles to win the World Stinging Nettle-Eating Championship in 2006.

Rhubarb leaves contain a poison called *oxalic acid* that irritates the gut and causes kidney damage. Luckily, they taste pretty foul so it's unlikely anyone would eat enough to poison themselves.

Californian Olivia Chanes felt something metallic in the hot dog she was eating. An x-ray showed that she had swallowed a 9 millimetre (one-third of an inch) bullet.

Pickled turkey gizzard is a traditional dish in some parts of the midwestern United States.

The strong smell of popular Chinese dish *stinky tofu* comes from it being fermented for as long as six months. It is sometimes black... even more appetizing!

British farmer Giles Peare is quite happy to snack on the slugs he finds on his farm. He thinks fried worms are tasty too.

11th-century Egyptians resorted to cannibalism when the Nile failed to flood for eight years in a row, causing a famine.

In the year 2000, food manufacturer Heinz produced tomato ketchups that were green, blue and purple. Everyone was quite happy with red, thank you, and the impostor sauces were discontinued.

Some traditional cheese-making procedures involve regular cleaning of the cheese's surface to rinse away the tiny cheese mites that feast on it.

In the Philippines, the eyes are considered the tastiest part of a steamed fish. Suck out the gloop and spit out the hard cornea.

British celebrity chef James Martin tried to make Brussels sprouts more appealing in 2004 by creating recipes for sprout ice cream, a sprout smoothie and a 'sproutini' cocktail.

Ever heard of a vegetable injury? The *cardoon* is a type of artichoke with a stalk that is covered in spines that can become lodged in the skin.

Severed heads, amputated limbs and internal organs went on display in a Thai bakery. The realistic-looking macabre items were made out of bread by art student Kittiwat Unarrom.

In traditional Italian cooking, a piece of sharpened horse's leg bone called a *spinto* is used to test whether a ham is cooked.

Cow's milk contains tiny amounts of pus and blood cells. If you're lucky, you might get some traces of antibiotics too.

The *death cap* is one of the world's most toxic mushrooms. Because it looks similar to edible mushrooms, it accounts for 50 per cent of all mushroom-poisoning cases. Symptoms include coma, jaundice and even death.

The edible part of a jackfruit is surrounded with sticky, white latex goo that clings to the fingers. Those in the know oil their hands before preparing one!

Japanese soldiers killed and ate eight American soldiers in 1945. They were later hanged for doing so.

Indian delicacy Bombay duck is, in fact, dried lizardfish. It's also known as *bummalo* and is so pongy that it has to be transported in airtight containers!

The Cambodian town of Skuon is known as Spiderville, famous for its dish of fried tarantula. The huge Thai zebra spiders are specially bred for food in holes in the ground.

Oranges imported into Europe from Israel in 1978 had been purposely contaminated with mercury by terrorists.

In 1951, the townspeople of French town Pont-Saint-Esprit were made ill by *pain maudit* (cursed bread) that made many of them psychotic. The grain used to make the flour was affected by *ergot*, a hallucinogenic fungus.

Popular British bar snack *pork scratchings* are bits of deep fried pig skin… some with hair still attached.

Gelatine (also known as E441) is made by boiling up animal skin, cartilage and bone for hours on end. It is added to a range of foods such as gummy sweets and jelly.

New York Times journalist William Buehler Seabrook obtained a chunk of fresh human meat from a hospital so that he could cook and eat it for research. He said it tasted like veal.

*Pets-de-nonne* (nun's farts) are delicate Canadian cinnamon rolls. Nuns don't fart, surely?

Red whelks can sometimes be mistaken for edible whelks, but their saliva is highly toxic. If eaten, they will cause blurred vision and paralysis.

Around 50,000 horses are slaughtered each year in the US to be exported for meat.

Death Row prisoner Kenny Richey wrote his own cookbook based on his prison experiences. His *Death Row Recipes* book includes a fish toastie that is warmed up on a radiator.

At least 16,000 children die around the world each day from hunger-related causes.

British man Les Lailey celebrated his Golden Wedding anniversary with wife Beryl by opening… a 50-year-old can of chicken! The whole jellied chicken had been in their wedding day hamper.

**Camel meat has been eaten in some parts of the world for centuries – the hump is apparently the best part.**

**Mould on decaying food can be white, green, brown, black, red or pink.**

Police seized 30 tonnes (66,138 pounds) of rotten meat from a rat-infested London warehouse in 2003. The illegal meat that was allegedly destined for human consumption included decomposing lambs' brains, goat carcasses, gizzards and cows' feet.

**The Papuan Korowai tribe practised cannibalism until around 1990.**

Can you guess what honey ants taste like? For a tasty bush tucker snack, just track down a nest, take an ant by the head and munch its sweet body.

**Chakna is a spicy Indian stew made with goat stomach and a sprinkling of other tasty animal parts.**

North-eastern Thai dish *yum khai mod daeng* is red ant egg salad. You can have extra ants if you ask nicely.

A 330-year-old cookery book found stored in a trunk in Derby, England, contained a section entitled 'A la mode ways of dressing the head of any beast'. It also gave recipes for marinated conger eel and hare mince pies.

**Filipino fermented fish *bagoong terong* smells like raw sewage!**

Chocolate is toxic to dogs, cats, horses and parrots, because their bodies cannot break down the chemical *theobromine* that comes from cocoa beans. If they eat too much, they can suffer from vomiting, diarrhoea and muscle spasms.

Toxic mushrooms such as the pure white *Destroying Angel* contain poison that destroys the liver and kidneys.

A British farmer added carrots to his cows' diet, but their milk turned pink! He solved the problem by importing white carrots from France.

Natural sausage casings are made from animal intestines.

The bacteria used for fermenting *Limburger* cheese are the same as the bacteria found on human skin that cause body odour. The monks who originally created the cheese used to pound it with their bare feet!

A family in Virginia opened their box of fried chicken to find a whole battered chicken's head inside!

A Florida jogger survived for four days on swamp water and leaves when he was trapped waist-deep in mud after taking a shortcut while out running.

Britain's first ever crocodile farm was set up in Cambridgeshire, England, where crocodiles are bred for food. The farmer helpfully says that the meat 'tastes like crocodile'.

The main ingredient in pepper spray is *capsaicin*, which comes from fiery chilli peppers. The spray causes tears, pain, coughing and temporary blindness.

Caffeine is a plant substance that paralyzes and kills insects. It is found in chocolate, cola, tea and coffee and is a central nervous system stimulant. Large amounts of caffeine can cause an irregular heartbeat, insomnia and muscle twitching.

65 million guinea pigs are eaten in Peru each year!

Beef tripe is from the first three of a cow's four stomachs: the *rumen* makes smooth tripe, the *reticulum* gives honeycomb tripe and book tripe comes from the *omasum*.

*Elephant ears* are a popular snack in the United States. Fortunately, they are not animal parts but pieces of fried dough sprinkled with sugar.

Shaw's Bistro and International Tapas Bar was the first restaurant in Scotland to serve rattlesnake, crickets and locusts.

An Edinburgh woman stopped eating her McDonald's cheeseburger when she noticed a huge spider in the box. When she looked inside the burger, there was another one in there too! The company issued an apology for the incident.

*Asafoetida* is a stinky spice that comes from plant sap and is also known as devil's dung or devil's dirt. It smells revolting as a powder but tastes delicious when cooked.

A traditional way to make African *amasi* (soured milk) was to leave unpasteurized milk out in the sun to fester for a couple of days!

Fried-brain sandwiches are a popular snack in some parts of the US.

Dark green-brown *grass jelly* is used in desserts and drinks in China and Southeast Asia. It really is jelly with grass in it.

Dozens of London residents were struck down by *diarrhetic shellfish poisoning* in 1998 after eating mussels from two of the capital's restaurants. It was the first case of the poisoning for 30 years.

Stinging nettles are a nutritious food and a little steaming gets rid of the sting. Nettle soup, anyone?

A robber was pelted with chicken drumsticks by staff when he tried to hold up a take-away at gunpoint in Sussex, England. He fled empty-handed.

*Rennet* is an enzyme taken from slaughtered calves' stomachs that is used in some traditionally- made cheeses to make them solid.

Tests on 2000-year-old faeces discovered in Roman military toilets unearthed in Scotland, showed that soldiers had enjoyed a meal made with eggs.

In medieval times, cow and deer innards were known as *umbles*. Umble pie was a popular dish among the lower classes and it's thought that this is where the phrase 'to eat humble pie' came from.

Large amounts of liquorice can cause liver damage. It can increase the amounts of the hormone *cortisol* in the liver, which raise blood pressure and blood sugar levels.

Swedish King Eric XIV was fatally poisoned by a bowl of arsenic-laced pea soup whilst in prison.

**Sipunculid worm jelly** is a delicacy in Xiamen, China. The marine worm burrows in sand and is known for its tentacled mouth.

A 2003 investigation by the British Coffee Association found that some coffees sold in Britain were contaminated with coffee bean mould, stones, twigs and 'floor sweepings'.

*Devon colic* was a type of lead poisoning suffered by people in Devon, England, after drinking the local cider in the 17th century. The cider presses were made of lead and lead shot was used to clean them.

Japanese fermented soya beans *nattou* come in a tacky goo that forms webby strings when pulled apart. They stink of blue cheese too!

*Slátur* is an Icelandic dish made by filling sheep stomachs with blood and fat.

The natural colour of margarine is grey, so yellow colouring is added to make it look more appetizing. It is illegal to sell margarine with colouring in Quebec.

Low quality cod liver oil smells of rotten fish and rancid oil. It tastes pretty yucky too!

Pokeweed leaves retain some of their poisonous toxins after being boiled. Despite this, poke salad remains a popular dish in the southern United States.

Black corn fungus, known as *huitlacoche*, is a delicacy in Mexico. The mould grows in damp corn after rain and makes the kernels swell up into big, deformed blobs.

The black stone in the *sapodilla* fruit has a hook at one end and can stick to the throat if swallowed.

Antarctic explorers Douglas Mawson and Xavier Mertz got severe vitamin A poisoning from eating husky liver after they lost their food supplies in a crevasse.

Grilled chicken gizzards are a popular street food in many Southeast Asian countries.

Lard is pig fat. Much of the lard sold in supermarkets is treated with bleaching and deodorising agents.

*Tripas* is a popular taco and burrito filling in Mexico. It's not tripe, but fried beef intestines.

Baltic herring is fermented for months to make a Swedish dish called *surströmming*. The fermentation process continues after canning, so the tin explodes on opening! It also releases a pungent liquid that surrounds the rotten fish.

Peanuts can be contaminated with a toxic mould called *aspergillus flavus*.

The thorny durian fruit from Southeast Asia has such a pungent odour (likened to stale vomit and rotten eggs) that it is banned from being taken into hotels and on public transport!

British man Brian Duffield can eat a whole raw onion in 1 minute 29 seconds.

After tasting his own '16 Million Reserve' super-hot chilli powder, Blair Lazar's tongue was swollen and painful for several days. His New Jersey company Extreme Foods makes fiery sauces with names like 'Mega Death'.

*Jumiles* are bitter-tasting stinkbugs that are used in Mexican sauces and taco fillings.

Boiled animal gunk *gelatine* is used by some synchronized swimmers to keep their hair in place as it does not dissolve in cold water.

'Green tripe' is usually brown or grey and refers to unwashed tripe. Tripe needs to be meticulously cleaned before you can eat it... if you really want to, that is.

The rennet used in the Brazilian cheese *queijo coalho* comes from guinea pig stomach linings.

**Hog *maw*** is a Pennsylvanian German dish of pig's stomach stuffed with sausage and potatoes, traditionally eaten on New Year's Day.

*Anisakis* is a worm that lives in fish. It is destroyed by extreme temperatures but a person who eats raw, salted or pickled fish that is infected will contract *anisakiasis*: severe stomach pain and vomiting will follow and larvae may be coughed up.

Mexican delicacy *chapulines* are fried grasshoppers. The grasshoppers must be thoroughly cooked as they often carry worms that can also infest humans.

*Menudo* and *mondongo* are South American stews made with slow-cooked diced tripe, sometimes with trotters added. Nicaraguan folklore says the stew has healing powers.

Microbial rennet is used in cheesemaking as an alternative to animal rennet and is made from fermented mould. Mmm, much tastier.

An Ohio woman felt something gristly in her mouthful of salad at a restaurant and was horrified to discover that it was a human fingertip, complete with nail! The chef had sliced it off whilst chopping the salad and had rushed off to hospital without it.

Popular South American soft drink *Inca Kola* looks like urine and tastes like bubble gum.

*Makchang is* a Korean dish of grilled pig's large intestine.

Yellow food colourings *tartrazine* and *Sunset Yellow FCF* are derived from coal tar, which is the sludge left over when coal is made into coke. Both are banned in Norway but widely used elsewhere.

*Shkembe chorba* is a Bulgarian soup made with beef tripe and milk.

# Gruesome Animal Facts

The fearsome coconut crab can crack coconuts with its mighty pincers and has a leg span of up to 1 metre (3 feet). The land crab is also nicknamed the 'robber crab', as it has been known to steal shiny objects from houses and tents.

A dung beetle can move a ball of manure that is hundreds of times heavier than its own weight.

A hippopotamus will spin its tail while defecating to mark as much territory as possible with its faeces.

Blister beetles secrete a poison that leaves a painful blister on the skin.

A woman tried on a pair of jeans in an Okinawa shop, only to be stung in the leg by a scorpion that was hiding inside them! Although the sting was not fatal, the woman was hospitalized for several days.

Only female midges bite you and will slurp up your blood for up to four minutes.

The star-nosed mole in North America looks like its nose just exploded! It has 22 wriggly pink tentacles on the end of its snout, which it uses to detect and eat prey in a matter of milliseconds.

Forty kamikaze birds crashed into windows and broke their necks in Vienna after becoming drunk on fermented berries.

The fangs of the Australasian funnel-web spider are so sharp that they have been known to penetrate fingernails and soft shoes.

Some cockroaches can run at over 5 kilometres (3 miles) per hour, travelling 50 times their body length each second. If you could do that, you could run faster than a racing car!

A *zoonosis* is any infectious disease that can be transferred between animals and people.

A bear shot by a hunter in Canada in 2006 was found to be a grizzly-polar bear hybrid, the first ever documented. Suggested names in the media for the unusual bear have been a 'pizzly' or a 'grolar bear'. The hunter kept the bear's carcass as a trophy.

Some birds swallow stones or grit to help break up the food in their stomachs and then regurgitate them later.

A pond in Hamburg was dubbed the 'pond of death' after hundreds of its toads mysteriously exploded, scattering entrails more than 3 metres (10 feet) away.

The *slow worm* is a legless lizard that can shed its tail if attacked.

Authorities in Iowa investigating complaints by neighbours discovered that a house contained 350 snakes and 500 assorted rodents. Only six illegal snakes were removed, as the animals were well looked-after.

Animal manure produces heat as it decomposes. It has been known for large piles of manure to burst into flames.

Baboons have rough, nerveless callouses on their bottoms so that they can sit anywhere in comfort!

The *death's head hawkmoth* has a skull-shaped pattern on its back. It is believed in many cultures that it brings bad luck if it flies into a house.

Vixens let out a long, eerie wail that sounds like a crying baby during the breeding season.

Some spiders spit special sticky goo at their prey so that it's literally glued to the spot.

A golden retriever in California gave birth to a puppy with green fur. Its owner named the puppy Wasabi, which is a green Japanese condiment made with horseradish.

If agitated, the fierce *Tasmanian devil* (the world's largest carnivorous marsupial) releases a foul odour.

A pinecone shortage in eastern Russia drove a gang of ravenous squirrels to attack and eat a stray dog.

Hollywood kangaroo Feznik had plastic surgery to reconstruct his lip after he was attacked by a wolf.

A 'sausage fly' is actually a male driver ant with a bloated, sausage-shaped abdomen.

Some fish in Antarctica have white blood! This is because their blood has very low levels of the chemical that makes blood red (*haemoglobin*) and contains natural antifreeze to stop them freezing in the icy waters.

**The bite of a hyena is so powerful that it can crush bone.**

A naturist in Australia received burns to 18 per cent of his body when he poured petrol down a hole and set fire to it in an attempt to get rid of a deadly funnel-web spider.

Birds do not urinate. Their urine and faeces are all mixed together to make one sloppy dropping.

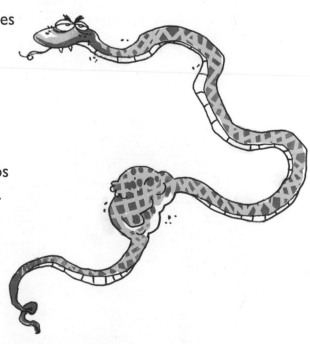

The spiny Australian lizard *thorny devil* will put its head between its front legs if threatened. A second, false head then pops up for the predator to munch on instead.

Lurking beneath the cute-looking *fluffy puss caterpillar*'s soft hairs are poisonous spines. When touched, the spines break off and get lodged in the skin, causing intense pain, numbness, blisters and a rash.

A Kenyan elephant that slipped into a septic tank whilst trying to eat bananas on a farm was then killed and eaten by villagers.

Bored monkeys will throw their faeces at anyone who happens to be passing!

The *wheel bug* has a cog shape on its back and its bite causes agonizing pain that can last for up to six hours.

Dogs love a bit of fresh tripe, even if the cow's stomach still has the remains of the cow's last meal stuck to it.

Camels have three eyelids. They need them as protection against sun and sand.

The eyes of the *golden mole* are covered with skin and fur. The mole lives in the desert and only comes out at night, so it has no need for eyes anyway. It looks like a golden hairball with legs!

The male duck-billed platypus has a sharp poisonous spur on its hind foot that can inflict severe pain on humans.

Scotsman David Evans was sentenced to six months' imprisonment for using a wet fish as an offensive weapon. He had slapped a passer-by round the face with it.

*Green muscardine* disease is a fungus that kills insects. The spores enter the insect and grow inside it, eventually covering the insect's outer body with green mould.

Many fly maggots eat dead flesh, but those of the screw-worm fly eat healthy flesh. If they infest an animal or human wound, they burrow in and destroy the healthy tissue around it, making the wound far worse.

A man was fined 25,000 Australian dollars (£10,409) after hiding six rare birds' eggs in his underwear and trying to smuggle them out of Sydney airport.

A German shepherd dog was successfully trained to sniff out sheep droppings that were infected with worms on an Australian sheep farm.

If a newt loses a leg, it just grows a new one!

British sunbather Sally Brown was almost killed when a calf fell from the cliff-side field 15 metres (50 feet) above and landed on the beach beside her.

Locust swarms cause traffic accidents in hot countries when cars skid on all the squashed ones!

A kangaroo can disembowel an attacking dog with its hind legs as it grips with its forepaws.

The Saharan desert ant can survive in temperatures of over 50 degrees Celsius (122 degrees Fahrenheit) and feeds on other insects that have frazzled in the heat.

A woman found a plastic lunch box in an Edinburgh street and opened it to find it was full of baby boa constrictors. Snake sandwich, anyone?

A pair of pigs in northern Italy became so enormous that they could not be moved and had to be taken from their sty in pieces. The pigs weighed 200 kilograms (440 pounds) each.

Fire ants are so called because a bite from one feels like a nasty burn on your skin.

British artist Damien Hirst pickled a shark measuring 4.3 metres (14 feet) in more than 900 litres (200 gallons) of formaldehyde. He called his work *The Physical Impossibility of Death in the Mind of Someone Living.*

Lizardfish have sharp teeth on their tongues. Ouch!

Eastern European peasants used to make wound dressings out of spiders' webs. In fact, spider silk has antiseptic properties, so it wasn't such a bad idea.

*Click beetles* are so called because they leap high into the air with a loud 'click' sound. Some of them glow in the dark, too.

Royal Bengal tigers have the longest canine teeth of all big cats, measuring an average of 10 centimetres (4 inches). The tigers frequently attack and eat people in the Sundarbans region of India and Bangladesh.

Cow dung sets hard in hot, dry countries and also contains a natural mosquito repellent, so is sometimes used to line rustic floors and walls. Caked cow dung is also used as a fuel when cooking.

The female golden silk orb-weaver spider is at least five times bigger than the male. She's definitely the boss!

The olive baboon has olive green skin.

US researchers discovered that *cottonmouth snake* venom was extremely effective at removing blood stains from white clothes.

Chinese genetic scientists have developed pigs that glow in the dark. The spooky porkers were created using injections of fluorescent green protein into the pig embryos.

Christmas Island is plagued with yellow crazy ants. These are aggressive ants that nest anywhere, form supercolonies with several queens and eat anything that moves, including birds, reptiles and even crabs!

The Peruvian booby bird uses its own droppings to make its nest.

*Stargazer* fish have two large poisonous spines on their backs and can also deliver electric shocks.

The Amazonian giant centipede can grow to more than 30 centimetres (1 foot) long and has claws that secrete toxic venom.

Children at a nursery in Weston-super-Mare, England, were alarmed to see a three-headed, six-legged mutant frog creep out of their pond. They were told off for fibbing when they got home.
(Only kidding!)

A Labrador dog was badly injured when it tried to lick up biscuit crumbs that had fallen into a home paper shredder in Scotland. The shredder was activated, trapping the poor pooch's tongue.

**Elephants have been known to stay standing up after they have died!**

*Garra rufa* fish are used in some health spas to treat skin disorders. People sit in pools full of the 'doctor fish' and wait for their dead skin and scabby bits to be nibbled away.

A hunter from the Basque village of Epelette was shot in the hip when one of his dogs stood on a loaded gun in the back of his car.

**The Barents Sea is teeming with monster Kamchatka crabs. The gigantic crustaceans can measure more than 1 metre (3 feet) from claw to claw and can weigh up to 12 kilograms (25 pounds).**

The African *zorilla* could be the smelliest creature on the planet. The pong secreted from its anal glands can be detected one kilometre (half a mile) away.

A vet was hospitalized with hydrogen sulphide poisoning after entering a cottage that had 20 cats locked inside. The toxic fumes were from the cats' faeces.

When a male lion takes over another lion's pride, he will kill any cubs so that he can later replace them with his own. Not very good step-parents!

Kangaroo manure has been used to make environmentally friendly paper in Tasmania.

The carrion beetle loves a tasty snail as a snack. It squirts digestive juices over the shell and then sucks out the snail's body. Delicious!

The jewel wasp lays its egg inside a cockroach, using a paralyzing sting to keep it still. The hatched larva then munches on the cockroach's internal organs until it becomes a wasp and bursts out.

A giant catfish in a park lake in Germany became known as 'Kuno the killer' after it jumped out and ate a Dachshund puppy whole!

British man Michael Fitzgerald needed plastic surgery on his legs and arm after he was attacked by a badger at his home in Evesham, England. The badger attacked four more people before it was caught.

Some stinkbugs can spit their smelly goo as far as 30 centimetres (1 foot).

The New Zealand *huhu* beetle is otherwise known as a 'haircutter'. It has sharp hooks on its long legs and antennae, so if one lands in your hair and gets entangled you need a haircut to get it out!

Since the mid 1990s, many Tasmanian devils have died from *devil's facial tumour disease*, a mysterious illness in which large tumours around and inside the mouth prevent feeding, causing the animals to die of starvation.

A cow called Punch urinated on British celebrity Bill Oddie while he was doing a live broadcast from a farm in Scotland.

The Australian navy boarded an Indonesian ship that was drifting off the northwest coast and found that there was no crew but 3 tonnes (6,614 pounds) of rotting mackerel and tuna onboard.

A strange-smelling suitcase abandoned at Amsterdam airport was found to contain 2,000 baboons' noses. It's believed the animal parts, en route from Nigeria to the United States, would have been used in traditional medicine.

*Glassfish* are transparent so you can peer in and see their bones and internal organs!

Wild boar hair was used to make toothbrushes before more hygienic, synthetic bristles were invented.

Cow parts caused traffic chaos when a meat lorry crashed near San Francisco and scattered its cargo across the freeway.

*Cone snails* or *cone shells* kill their prey by firing a poisonous harpoon from their mouths. Their venom is highly toxic to humans, who unknowingly pick up the pretty shells. The harpoon is so sharp that it has been known to penetrate wetsuits.

Hyenas have extremely acidic digestive juices. This means they can digest every bit of their prey, including teeth, hooves and horns.

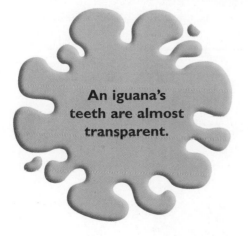

An iguana's teeth are almost transparent.

South African man Abel Manamela took revenge on the bank that repossessed his car by releasing deadly adders into the building. As a cleaner was bitten by one of the snakes, he was charged with attempted murder.

A *scatologist* is a person who studies animal faeces.

The polar bears in Singapore Zoo turned green in 2004. Their change in colour was due to a type of algae growing in their hollow hair shafts.

Honeybees will surround any intruder in their colony, such as a hornet, and vibrate their bodies. This creates so much heat that the invader is cooked to death!

British anti-litter campaigners have warned that junk food litter is creating monstrous 'super-pigeons' that rely on waste to survive.

**Cows produce 200 times more saliva than humans. What a lot of dribble!**

A sparrow was shot dead in a hall in Leeuwarden, Holland, after sending more than 23,000 dominoes tumbling over. The dominoes had been set up for a world record attempt and the organizers were a little annoyed.

Rat's urine often carries *Weil's disease*, a serious and sometimes fatal infection that causes jaundice and kidney damage. It is usually contracted after contact with infected water.

A two-headed turtle hatched at a turtle refuge in Costa Rica. It was believed that the deformity was caused by ocean pollution.

Bad-tempered hippos kill more people in Africa than any other big-game safari animal, including crocodiles. They usually charge and trample victims, but have also been known to bite a man's head off!

**A giraffe's blue-black tongue is *prehensile*, meaning it can grasp things. It can be as long as 60 centimetres (2 feet)!**

The venom of recluse spiders is *necrotic*, which means a bite will result in a large, open sore that will take months to heal and may require skin grafts.

The word bonfire comes from 'bone fire', since ritual fires usually involved the burning of animal bones to ward off evil spirits.

Slugs produce two sorts of mucus: one is thin and watery, the other is thick and sticky.

British artist Chris Ofili is known for using an unusual ingredient in his paintings: elephant dung!

The fat-tailed scorpion is responsible for most human deaths from scorpion stings. Although its venom is less toxic than that of the deathstalker scorpion, it injects more into its victim.

The violet gland is a tail gland in foxes and badgers used for scent marking. The gland's secretion is fluorescent in ultraviolet light and although it contains the same substance as violet flowers, it is far more concentrated and smells really nasty.

South African woman Elsie van Tonder had her nose bitten off by a seal when she tried to help it back into the sea. There's gratitude for you.

Stampeding wild pigs killed Indonesian footballer Mistar during a 1995 training session.

**Bombardier beetles protect themselves from a predator by blasting an explosive fart of boiling hot poisonous gas in its direction.**

A common cause of pet ferret deaths is the reclining chair. The ferret snuggles up under the chair when it is reclined and then gets squished when its unknowing owner puts the seat back in position.

Bee sting therapy is sometimes used to treat conditions such as multiple sclerosis and arthritis. Bee venom contains a substance called *melittin*, which is anti-inflammatory (reduces swelling). Bees are pressed on to the patient and allowed to sting.

Animal dandruff is called *dander*.

British performance artist Paul Hurley wrapped himself in clingfilm and wriggled about in a soggy field nibbling soil for nine days. He called his performance *Becoming Earthworm*.

The Mexican mountain village of Atascaderos was plagued by rats that had learnt to avoid poison. It was estimated that there were 250,000 rats roaming the village.

The hairy-handed crab has hairy pads on its nippers where food particles collect. When it's hungry, the crab nibbles on its hairy claws!

The tiny black and white *minute pirate bug* bites by sticking its beak-like snout into the skin.

*Pilobolus* is a fungus that grows on herbivore dung and breaks it down. Although less than 1 centimetre (1/4 inch) tall, it can launch its *sporangium* (spores) up to 2 metres (6 feet) away. The herbivore eats it with the grass and the cycle begins again.

The skin and feathers of *pitohui* birds are poisonous. Touching them will cause numbness and tingling.

When animal control officers in Virginia investigated complaints of a foul smell coming from the house of pensioner Ruth Kneuven, they found over 300 cats, more than 80 of which were dead.

A snow scorpion is used to such low temperatures that one would die from heat exhaustion if you held it in your hand. As if you'd want to!

The number of cane toads in Australia reached a record 200 million in 2006. The army was called in to help control the plague of poisonous amphibians.

Rats cannot burp or vomit – but they can spread disease.

Three Peruvian fishermen who were lost at sea for 59 days survived by eating turtle meat and drinking turtle blood.

**Kangaroos cover themselves with saliva to keep cool in the scorching Australian sun.**

Research by scientists Dr Ben Wilson and Dr Bob Batty revealed that herrings fart frequently… but only at night!

**A skunk can squirt its sulphurous spray up to 3 metres (10 feet) away, leaving its victim with stinging eyes and gasping for air.**

Porcupines looking for salt have been known to eat tool handles and clothes because of the salty human sweat on them.

When Romanian Gyenge Lajos complained to the authorities about a gas-like smell, investigators soon discovered the cause: a dead cow in the man's apartment. It had been a gift from a friend and the man was cutting pieces from it as he needed them.

The Chow is the only breed of dog that has a purple-black tongue.

South American silk moth caterpillars are extremely venomous. They are covered with hairs that release anticoagulant venom on contact, so that an affected person can bleed to death.

The largest known jellyfish is the Arctic *lion's mane* jellyfish. The biggest ever found was washed up in Massachusetts Bay; its body was a huge 2.3 metres (7 feet 6 inches) wide and its tentacles were 36.5 metres (120 feet) long.

Customs officials at Melbourne airport were suspicious when they heard splashing sounds coming from a woman's skirt. Further investigations revealed that she was smuggling 51 live tropical fish in a water-filled apron.

The colossal squid is even scarier than the giant squid; its suckers are full of swivelling hooks.

The giant squid has hundreds of suckers and inside each one is a ring of sharp teeth, so it can suck on to its prey and perforate it at the same time.

A monstrous wild hog dubbed 'Hogzilla' was shot in the state of Georgia in 2004. It was 2.4 metres (8 feet) long with 23 centimetres (9 inch) tusks.

The male funnel-web spider is extremely aggressive. It will actively attack a person by lunging and will bite repeatedly.

A decomposing sperm whale exploded in Taiwan as it was being transported for a post mortem, showering nearby shops and cars with blood and blubber. A natural build-up of gas inside the beached whale was to blame.

A giraffe's heart is 60 centimetres (2 feet) long and weighs around 11 kilograms (25 pounds).

The red 'blood sweat' that a hippopotamus secretes contains sunscreen and antibacterial agents. The secretion starts off clear and changes colour to red, then brown.

The Australian *fierce snake* has the most toxic snake venom in the world. A single bite contains enough venom to kill up to 100 adult humans.

Once a year, the roads and paths of Christmas Island are covered with red crabs that are scuttling from their burrows towards the sea to lay their eggs. There are so many that cars just have to drive over them if they're going to get anywhere.

Jokers who let a rat loose in a British McDonald's branch were taken aback when the restaurant manager beat it to death with a broom in front of customers.

The cassowary bird's dagger-like middle claw is 12 centimetres (5 inches) long and razor sharp, enabling the bird to disembowel an enemy with a single kick.

Whales vomit every 7–10 days to get rid of any indigestible items they may have swallowed. It's not known if they warn any nearby sea creatures what's coming.

Hard ticks (ticks that have shells) that burrow in to people's skin can spread *Rocky Mountain spotted fever*, originally known as black measles. It causes fever, muscle pain, headache and a rash. If untreated, it can be fatal.

When a kodiak bear kills a deer, it will eat the internal organs first.

Queen Victoria's coronation ring was made for her little finger, but the Archbishop insisted on forcing it on to her ring finger to follow tradition. The Queen was in agony during the ceremony and it took two hours to get the ring off afterwards.

King George II died of a heart attack while he was on the toilet.

Roman gladiators in training were fed spoonfuls of ash by their trainers, in the belief that it built up the body. So don't moan again about eating your greens...

Scottish aristocrat Alexander Hamilton, the tenth Duke of Hamilton, wanted to be mummified after his death and so bought an ancient Egyptian sarcophagus. When he died in 1852, his legs had to be shortened to fit his body inside it!

Charles VI of France suffered from a mental illness that made him believe his body was made of glass. He even put metal rods in his clothes so he wouldn't shatter.

Criminals in ancient times would be sewn inside a rotting animal skin and then tied to a tree, where they would be eaten alive by vultures.

French watchmaker Robert Hubert was hanged for starting the Great Fire of London, but it was later discovered that he arrived in the city two days after it broke out. He confessed to the crime, so was either tortured or a bit mad.

16th-century combs were often made from elephant's tusks (ivory).

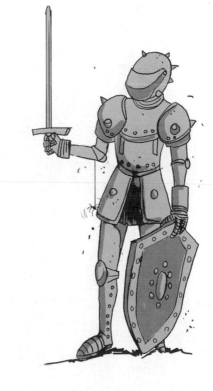

When he was badly injured in the First World War, Ernest Hemingway stemmed the flow of blood with cigarette ends.

Poor Victorians used to mix flour with water for baby food. Unsurprisingly, babies were often sick in those days.

During the 18th century, fur used for hats was soaked in a solution containing high levels of mercury. The toxic vapours caused mercury poisoning, a symptom of which was *dementia* – that's where the phrase 'as mad as a hatter' came from.

Mircea, the brother of Vlad (when he was just Vlad and hadn't yet started impaling) was blinded with hot stakes and buried alive by his enemies.

English King Edward the Martyr was killed by his stepmother in 979 AD. She offered him a drink and then stabbed him in the back as he sat and drank it.

Early candles were made from cow fat or whale blubber.

Scottish writer Sir Thomas Urquhart literally died laughing! This cause of death is known as 'fatal hilarity'.

The guillotine is associated with the French Revolution, but a similar device called the *Maiden* was used in Scotland long before that. It was introduced by Regent James Douglas, fourth Earl of Morton, who ended up being executed by it himself for treason.

Glue used thousands of years ago was made by boiling up animal hooves and leaving the goo to set. You had to break the hooves up into chunks first.

Viking funerals often involved putting the corpse in a boat and setting fire to it.

Many men and horses died during the chariot races popular with the ancient Greeks and Romans. Death was all part of the fun in those days!

Old shipwrecks are often riddled with *shipworms*, snaky molluscs that burrow into the wood and chomp away at it.

Most medieval manuscripts were written on bits of stretched out calf-skin, known as *vellum*.

The Tower of London's famous ravens all died of shock during the Second World War bombings of London. A new lot were put in place before the Tower reopened.

Russian writers Alexander Pushkin and Mikhail Lermontov both died from gunshot wounds after fighting in duels.

An unusual duel to the death was fought in Paris in 1808: two Frenchmen shot at each other from hot air balloons until one balloon was shot down!

It was believed in the Middle Ages that if you had some of your enemy's hair, you had control over him (or probably just his head lice).

In 212 BC, 460 Chinese intellectuals who refused to burn their books during the Qin dynasty were buried alive for their defiance.

Animal blood was believed to have special powers and was often sprinkled on the statues of Norse gods. People taking part in these rituals would often shower themselves with the blood too!

**The first *bone china* was made with crushed ox bones.**

When Viking warlord Ragnar Lodbrok was defeated during a battle in England in 865, he was thrown into a pit of venomous snakes and bitten to death.

The deteriorating mummy of pharaoh Ramesses II was sent to Paris to be treated for a fungal infection (mould) in 1974. It was issued with a passport for transportation on which the occupation was stated as 'King (deceased)'.

English mathematician Alan Turing committed suicide by painting an apple with cyanide and eating it.

In 200 BC, Carthaginian soldiers pretended to flee their city and left behind wine laced with the toxic plant *mandrake*. Invading Romans guzzled the wine, only to be finished off by the returning soldiers while they were weakened by the poison.

King Harold was killed at the Battle of Hastings in 1066 by an arrow shot through his eye.

For two years after the Krakatoa volcano erupted in 1883, the moon appeared to be blue.

In the late 19th century, an Egyptian farmer discovered a tomb that was filled with thousands of mummified cats and kittens.

The hot summer and unprecedented levels of sewage in the Thames in 1858 led to The Great Stink – Londoners were almost knocked out by the foul smell.

There were hundreds of altars for animal sacrifices at the ancient Greek Olympics. The biggest of these was the Great Altar of Zeus, where the thighs of 100 oxen would be roasted for the gods. The other bits were used for a big banquet later.

*Black pox* was a symptom of smallpox, in which the skin took on a charred appearance, turning black and peeling off.

People afflicted with warts during the Middle Ages used to pay a wart-charmer to get rid of them.

Renaissance painters coated their canvases with rabbit-skin glue, made from boiling rabbit skins. It was all they could think of to prepare their paper for oil paints!

The *Scavenger's Daughter* was a 16th-century torture device that compressed the body until blood came out of the nose and ears.

1001 Gruesome Facts

During the embalming of Catherine of Aragon's body, her heart was found to be black. This led to fears that she had been murdered, but it is more likely that it was a form of cancer.

In the 8th century, Chinese poet Li Bai drowned in the Yangtze River when he drunkenly tried to touch the moon and fell in!

Before shoe polish was invented, people would make their shoes waterproof by rubbing them with a lump of sheep fat.

When the Bishop of Rochester's cook poisoned some guests, Henry VIII chose the punishment: the cook was boiled alive in his own pot!

Realizing that he had become extremely unpopular, King Henry I of Haiti shot himself with a silver bullet in 1820, rather than go through the indignity of a coup.

> **Men of the Iron Age were sometimes buried with their chariot...
> along with the poor horses that pulled it.**

*Ivory black* paint wasn't just any old black paint – it was made by burning an elephant's tusk, scraping off the black bits and mixing them with oil.

An English ship, *The Mary Rose,* sank in 1545. It wasn't recovered until 1982, when the remains of half the crew were found on board.

The victorious enemies of Roman emperor Valerian killed him by pouring molten gold down his throat.

German scientist Georg Richmann heard a thunderstorm in 1753 and rushed out to observe it. Lightning collided with his head, his shoes exploded and he died.

Italian dictator Benito Mussolini was expelled from school at the age of 11 for stabbing a schoolmate in the hand and poking a stick in another boy's eye.

On American ships, cats with extra toes were thought to bring good luck on voyages. In Europe, it was believed that cats with extra toes belonged to witches and should be destroyed!

People suffering from tuberculosis during the 17th century were thought to be vampires, since they were pale, had swollen, bloodshot eyes and coughed up blood.

In his later years, Chairman Mao Zedong had green teeth!

Arsenic was a popular murder weapon in the Middle Ages; as well as being tasteless and colourless, it resulted in the same symptoms as cholera and often went undetected.

In the late 19th century, most public places in the United States had *spittoons*, which were dishes for men to spit into. It was thought to be more hygienic than spitting on the floor.

Dutch artist Vincent van Gogh had such a bad diet (bread, coffee and absinthe) that his teeth were loose. He looked so scary, especially after he cut off part of his ear, that neighbours petitioned to have the *fou roux* – the mad redhead – removed.

**Whenever Kodiak natives (*Alutiiqs*) killed a bear, they would leave the head as a sign of respect for the spirit of the bears.**

Early thickeners for inks included the sludge from boiled-up donkey skins and insect faeces.

On realizing their impending defeat, several high-ranking Second World War Nazis killed themselves with cyanide salts. The poison would have quickly caused convulsions before death.

**Egyptian queen Cleopatra killed herself by purposely taking figs from a basket with venomous asp vipers in it. She kindly allowed two of her handmaidens to die with her.**

In 1849, two thousand English people died each week from cholera.

Tightly-laced corsets that were fashionable between the 16th and 18th centuries would squeeze the internal organs; the liver would be pressed against the ribs, the stomach was made smaller and the lungs would not be able to work properly, leading to a build-up of mucus and a persistent cough.

A medieval cure for just about anything was *cauterization*: the affected body part was burned with a hot poker.

The toxic plant *mandrake* was used as an early anaesthetic by the Romans to make patients drowsy, so they didn't feel a limb being amputated... quite as much!

The first American astronaut Alan Shepard had to urinate inside his spacesuit after his Mercury capsule flight was delayed for several hours.

*Acqua Toffana* was a deadly 17th-century Italian cocktail of arsenic, lead and *belladonna* (deadly nightshade). It was used mainly by women to get rid of their husbands.

The *blood eagle* was a particularly gruesome Viking method of murder. Whilst still alive, the victim's ribs would be cut and opened out, then the lungs would be removed.

For thousands of years, crushing by elephant was a common form of execution in parts of Asia.

After Prince Albert's death, Queen Victoria insisted that fresh clothes be laid out for him every day. This had to be done for forty years after he died.

The *retarius* Roman gladiator would catch his opponent in a huge lead-weighted net before moving in for the kill with a trident.

700 black bears were killed and skinned in order to make Busby hats for the soldiers at Queen Elizabeth II's coronation in 1953.

Victorian women rubbed a concoction of arsenic, vinegar and chalk into their skin in the belief that it kept their skin youthful. Wrinkles? Maybe not. Arsenic poisoning? Definitely!

**Brutal Roman Emperor Caracalla was assassinated by one of his own officers... while urinating at a roadside.**

Medieval foot soldiers used huge, sharp forks to spear passing knights and pull them off their horses.

Any Roman gladiators who tried to stop fighting would be prodded with hot pokers to spur them on again.

Bolshevik revolutionary Leon Trotsky was murdered by a blow to the skull with an ice axe from a Stalinist agent.

The ancient Phoenicians discovered that they could get purple-blue dye from the mucus of sea snails.

As long ago as 1000 BC, Indians inoculated themselves against smallpox by rubbing pus from the pustule of an infected person into a scratch on a healthy person. The Chinese did it by blowing powdered smallpox scabs up the noses of healthy people.

Part of Lincoln Park in Chicago was previously a cemetery. Although it was believed that graves had been moved, skeletons were still being discovered during construction work in the 1980s.

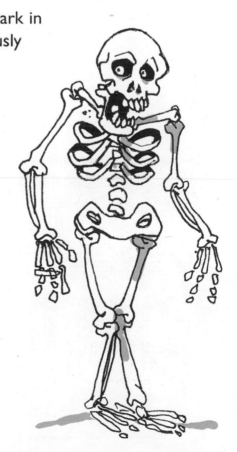

When Coca Cola was first invented in 1885, it was a medicine made with the illegal drug cocaine.

In ancient Greece, prisoners condemned to death were made to drink a solution made from the toxic plant *poison hemlock*. The most famous victim was the philosopher Socrates.

Mary Ann Cotton was a 19th-century serial killer who used arsenic to fatally poison up to 20 people, including her own husbands and children. She was hanged for the murders but died a slow, painful death after the hangman misjudged the dropping distance.

Holes in Viking long ships were plugged with a sticky mixture of tar and animal hair.

Part of a human skull discovered next to a pub car park in Crewe, England, was identified as being 700 years old. Fancy waiting that long to be served!

An ancient Persian method of execution, known as *the boats*, involved covering the condemned criminal in honey, tying him to a boat and leaving him on some stagnant, smelly water to be eaten alive by insects.

French king Charles I was killed by the single stroke of a *halberd*, an axe on a pole that was sharp enough to slice right through the helmet of his armour.

The *Death Railway* that linked Thailand and Burma was built by the Japanese during the Second World War. More than 100,000 labourers and prisoners of war died during its construction.

Unwilling to live under Caesar's rule, Roman statesman Cato the Younger tried to kill himself with his sword. He failed and was stitched up by a doctor, but then pulled the stitches out and ripped out his own intestines.

Research on Beethoven's hair showed that he died of lead poisoning. That's probably why he was as deaf as a post!

After the French ship *Medusa* ran aground in 1816, those who escaped on a raft resorted to cannibalism after four days adrift.

Early 19th-century Scottish surgeon Robert Liston could carry out an amputation in just 30 seconds. Since there were no anaesthetics in those days, it was just as well!

Murderous dictator Idi Amin, known as the Butcher of Africa, used a hotel in Kampala as his interrogation and torture centre.

After he was killed at the Battle of Trafalgar, Horatio Nelson's body was preserved in a barrel of brandy for transport to London. He wouldn't have been happy if he knew it was French!

American writer Sherwood Anderson died after swallowing a toothpick.

King Henry I of England's son William drowned when the *White Ship* sank in 1120. The ship's owner would have survived, but when he discovered the heir to the throne had died, he drowned himself – the King would have killed him anyway.

In 1936, Japanese microbiologist Shiro Ishii set up Unit 731, a secret compound in China where germ warfare experiments were carried out. Thousands of local people were killed in his tests by diseases such as bubonic plague, cholera and anthrax.

The earliest examples of tuberculosis were found in 17,000-year-old bison remains.

People who didn't escape the eruption of Vesuvius were trapped under deep ash. When their bodies decomposed, they left their shape behind in the ash. Plaster casts were made of the victims almost 2,000 years later.

Pope John XXI died in the newly built wing of his palace after his bedroom ceiling fell on him in 1277.

The great sword or long sword used in medieval battles was so big that it had to be held in both hands. It could chop off a limb, even through armour.

Henry II of France was killed during a jousting match when the sliver of a shattered lance pierced his eye and brain, coming out near his ear.

Ancient Romans used whips with pieces of bone or metal on the end. A plain old whip just wasn't nasty enough!

Chinese Prime Minister Li Si invented the *Five Pains* execution: a condemned prisoner had his nose, hand, foot and testicles cut off before being sawn in half. Li Si got his comeuppance, because he ended up being executed this way in 208 BC!

In 1920, Ray Chapman became the only Major League baseball player to have been killed by a pitch (a bowled ball). The sound of the ball hitting his skull was so loud that one player mistook it for the ball being hit with the bat and fielded it.

A lot of the ancient Greek Olympic events were done in the nude. (Try not to think of all those wobbly bits!)

So many people died from the Black Death that funerals were dispensed with and infected bodies were thrown into 'plague pits'. Pits were often filled with hundreds of corpses.

Women used to apply eye drops made from deadly nightshade to make their pupils bigger, in the belief that it made them look more beautiful. In fact, the toxic drops blurred their vision, increased their heart rate and if used often, caused blindness.

Rather than fall into enemy hands, Samurai warriors would commit suicide by *seppuku*, slicing open their stomachs with their sword in the belief that their spirit would be released.

Soviet leader Vladimir Lenin spent the last six years of his life with a bullet lodged in his neck, left there after an assassination attempt. He would never get through customs these days.

In 1936, the United States was hit by a deadly heatwave which killed around 20,000 people. The victims died of heat stroke and heat exhaustion when their body temperature soared out of control.

Sir Francis Drake died of *dysentery* (the mother of all diarrhoeas!).

The punishment for 17th-century French murderer Marquise de Brinvilliers was to be force-fed 9 litres (16 pints) of water before being beheaded. They burned her at the stake too, just to be sure.

The internal organs of ancient Egyptians were kept in vases called *canopic jars*, labelled with hieroglyphics and figures. The figure of the baboon-headed god *Hapy*, for example, would be painted on a jar containing the lungs.

As a boy, Spanish artist Salvador Dalí was horrified to find his pet bat dead and covered in ants. He later used ant images in much of his work.

In 18th-century France, it was traditional to remove and preserve the heart of dead monarchs.

A *trebuchet* was a kind of medieval sling weapon. It was used to fire boulders, dead animals, beehives and even severed heads over castle walls!

*Sweating sickness* was an infectious disease that killed thousands of people in Europe during the 15th and 16th centuries. Violent shivers and severe neck pain would be followed by excessive sweating and delirium.

Each newborn baby in the ancient Greek city of Sparta was bathed in wine and then taken to the elders, who would decide if it was strong enough to be reared. If not, it was left on a hillside to perish. That's one way to stop a baby crying!

Chinese Emperor Qin Shi Huang took mercury pills to give him eternal life. Unfortunately, they gave him mercury poisoning and killed him instead.

The unluckiest of gladiators had to fight as an *andabatus*. They were on horseback but were made to wear helmets with no eyeholes, so they couldn't see what was coming.

Abraham Lincoln's mother died after drinking milk from a cow that had eaten *white snakeroot*, a poisonous herb. *Milk sickness* killed many people in the 19th century.

Italian-French composer Jean-Baptiste de Lully stabbed himself in the foot with his long baton while conducting a work for Louis XIV. An abscess formed but he refused to have the gangrenous toe amputated, and later died of blood poisoning.

The *morning star* was a medieval club-like weapon with big spikes on the end. It was used to kill or wound the enemy with the double whammy of a heavy blow and a puncture attack.

Baking powders in the 19th century contained bone ash, the powder left over when animal bones were burned.

Nazi doctor Josef Mengele experimented with changes in eye colour by injecting chemicals into children's eyes.

Dutch artist Vincent van Gogh tried to commit suicide quickly by shooting himself in the chest. Unfortunately he only wounded himself and it took two more agonizing days for him to die.

The old English occupation of *dog whipper* involved sitting in a church with a whip and using it to get rid of any unruly dogs that might disrupt the service.

The decapitated head of Vlad the Impaler was sent to Istanbul, where the Sultan had it preserved in honey and put on display as proof of the brutal Romanian's death.

Between 50 and 100 million people died from flu during a pandemic in 1918–1919, wiping out entire towns in some countries. Symptoms included blueness in the face and coughing up blood.

A mini tsunami swept along the Bristol Channel, England, in 1607. Whole villages were swept away, with 2,000 people losing their lives.

Many medieval knights fighting in hot countries were known to have died of heat exhaustion, literally cooking inside their armour (especially the fatter ones!).

Josef Stalin was badly scarred by smallpox and had photographs touched up to hide the scars.

Following an argument over where English novelist Thomas Hardy should be laid to rest, his heart was buried in Dorset and his ashes in Westminster Abbey.

The dead body of King Harold II had to be identified in 1066 by the tattoos on his chest, as his face was so badly mutilated. The tattoos read 'England' and 'Edith'.

The last execution of a prisoner at the Tower of London was in 1941. German spy Josef Jakobs was shot by a firing squad of eight Scots Guards. As he already had a broken ankle, he was allowed to remain seated to receive his punishment in comfort!

During times of war, Japanese women would kill themselves before invading soldiers reached them. Using the method of *jigai*, they would cut their own throats.

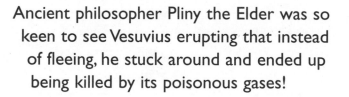

Ancient philosopher Pliny the Elder was so keen to see Vesuvius erupting that instead of fleeing, he stuck around and ended up being killed by its poisonous gases!

Mexican artist Frida Kahlo was impaled though the abdomen by an iron handrail in a bus crash when she was 18 years old.

*Anaemia* (iron deficiency) was common amongst ancient Egyptians. It was caused by bloodsucking parasites such as hookworm, which were rife in those times. A telltale sign of the illness is tiny holes in the mummies' eye sockets and skulls.

As a test of their masculinity, Spartans held competitions to see who could take the most flogging.

Some ancient Greek prisoners were executed in a *brazen bull*: they would be locked inside a brass sphere and a fire was lit underneath it, roasting the prisoner to death.

In ancient Roman funeral processions, jesters called *archimimes* were employed to walk behind the dead person and impersonate them (as they were when they were alive, obviously; a corpse impression wouldn't be that entertaining!).

During the Middle Ages, dead bodies that had to be transported over long distances were de-fleshed: skin, muscles and organs were cut away so that only the bones were left.

The punishment for killing (or trying to kill) a king in 17th-century France was to be tortured with hot pincers, molten wax and boiling oil before having the limbs torn off by horses. People would flock to watch it happening.

A 10th-century form of Chinese execution was called 'slow slicing' or 'death from a thousand cuts'. No prizes for guessing what that involved!

In 1586, Roman Catholic martyr Margaret Clitherow was arrested for harbouring Roman Catholic priests. She refused to confess or deny the charge in order to spare her children the trauma of a trial, so was executed by being crushed under stones.

English poet Ann Askew was the only woman to be tortured in the Tower of London. She was badly crippled by months of being stretched on a rack for her religious beliefs and was eventually burned at the stake.

One of the first sewers was the *Cloaca Maxima* in Rome. Open drains took sewage into the River Tiber, but sometimes the river currents caused backwash, sending all the stinky stuff back into the city.

Albert Einstein's brain was removed, sliced up and preserved in jars by pathologist Dr Thomas Harvey. He kept it for 43 years before giving it to McMaster University, Ontario.

**Faulty electrical wiring smells of rotten fish!**

**Burglars in Vienna fled when they found eight mummified heads in the basement flat they had broken into. The heads belonged to a dentist who was using them for research.**

Early polio vaccines contained ground-up monkey spinal cords and monkey kidney tissue.

Zoologists tell the age of a bear by sawing its tooth in half and counting the rings inside – just as you would with a tree!

The skull of a Tyrannosaurus Rex was up to 1.5 metres (5 feet) long. Human-sized animals would still be alive while they were being munched in its mouth.

Australian rainbow plants look pretty, but in fact they are insect traps: the sticky leaves act as natural flypaper and glue the insects to the spot. The more they struggle, the more stuck they become.

18th-century chemist Antoine Lavoisier gave oxygen its name, but ended up being deprived of it in a brutal way: he was beheaded during the French Revolution.

If you are right-handed, your left armpit will sweat more than your right. If you're left-handed, you're more likely to get those pit patches under your right arm.

Castor bean extract *ricin* is twice as deadly as cobra venom. It was used on an umbrella tip to murder Bulgarian dissident Georgi Markov.

When photographic flashes are used, eye pupils cannot close fast enough, so the blood-rich retinas are illuminated. That's what gives people that devilish red-eye look in some pictures.

*Stinkhorn* mushrooms reek of dung! This is to attract flies, which then go off with spores on their feet and spread them elsewhere.

Camels are able to completely seal their nostrils to stop sand going up their noses.

If you knock your friends out after eating garlic, it's down to garlic blood. The garlic pong travels in blood that supplies the lungs, transferring the smell to your breath.

A *chamois* is a type of goat. Lots of people polish their cars with chamois leathers – nice bits of goatskin.

Trans fats are man-made fats that are used for deep-frying and in processed foods. These nasty fats can lead to coronary heart disease by clogging up the body's arteries.

The smell made by rotten eggs, sewers and the worst farts is caused by a toxic, flammable gas called hydrogen sulphide.

When in danger, the sea cucumber will vomit out all its internal organs to distract the predator and escape. Then it just grows new ones!

The temperature of volcano lava can be as hot as 1200 degrees Celsius (2200 degrees Fahrenheit) – 12 times hotter than boiling water.

Ear infection otitis causes swelling and itching of the skin lining the ear canal. It can also make the ear produce a yucky, foul-smelling discharge.

Sea lice are gourmet guzzlers;
they feed on the mucus in fish gills.

Plastic surgeons sometimes
insert breast implants through
the belly button; it is cut open
and stretched, allowing the
surgeon to fit his whole arm
in before putting the implant
in place.

Many food
thickeners are made
from *carageenan* and
*gelatin* – that's seaweed
and animal hooves
to you and me.

The serious infection *salmonella* is in the
faeces of some birds and reptiles,
so make sure you wash your hands
after you've held your mate's pet iguana...

American Dr Charles Arntzen is
researching ways of creating fruits that
contain vaccines against disease.
A diphtheria banana might sound gross
but it's still better than an injection!

Hot tubs may look enticing, but they can harbour the bacteria that cause pneumonia-like infection Legionnaire's Disease, which is spread through contaminated evaporated water.

Ten per cent of all horseshoe crabs die just from being upside down. They cannot get back on their legs if flipped on to their backs and are washed ashore by rough seas.

In the US, most cases of rabies are caught not from dogs but from bat bites. If unvaccinated, people with rabies develop brain swelling and die within days.

*Jelly fungus* is a wibbly-wobbly mushroom. It tastes like soil but you can eat it if you want to.

A newborn elephant calf will snort to get rid of all the fluids in its trunk. Probably best to stand clear if you don't want to be showered with trunk gunk.

Tarantulas have claws at the end of their legs to grip prey with.

A *bezoar* is a stone found inside the intestines of hoofed animals. People used to put one in their drinks in the belief that it would neutralize any poison that was lurking there. It did no such thing, of course.

Tarantulas have irritating, barbed hairs on their backs called *urticating* hairs. Some can even fire these at predators.

The first filter-tipped cigarettes contained asbestos. As if they weren't deadly enough!

Chemical engineers have developed a spray-on skin. The special goo is designed to cover soldiers' wounds in war zones and can last for up to two weeks in mud and other nasty germ-filled environments.

The ozone layer that we need to protect us from the sun's harmful rays is actually made up of a stinky, poisonous gas. Lucky it's so high up then!

Indian Professor Syed Abdul Gafoor refused to bury his mother when she died. Instead, he had her body preserved in a glass case in his home until he died 20 years later and they were buried together. Not surprisingly, his wife had left him before then!

Octopuses have three hearts: two for pumping blood through the gills and one for pumping blood around the body.

Sewer workers need emergency breathing apparatus when amongst slow-flowing sewage, as it gives off high levels of methane gas and eggy sulphide smells.

In 2000, a study into the cleanliness of seats on the London Underground showed that a row of seats contained the remains of six mice, two large rats and one previously unheard of fungus.

Threadworm eggs are so tiny that you can't see them. They float in the air and can shoot up your nose uninvited – then they enter your stomach and hatch into little worms.

The Amazon ant steals eggs from other ant colonies. It covers the newly hatched ants in smelly substances called *pheromones* that make them think they're in the right colony and act as slaves to their new master.

Air that contains more than 50 per cent oxygen is toxic – breathing it in will cause lung damage.

American inventor Thomas Edison electrocuted several animals in his research on electricity. In 1903, he filmed the death by electrocution of a zoo elephant that had killed three people and the film was seen by many people across the US.

After a skin injury, scar tissue growth can get out of control and form a big, rubbery lump called a *keloid*.

In 2006, a crowd control device was patented that shoots a stream of slime at troublemakers to make them slide into submission.

The skin infection *ringworm* is not caused by a worm but by a fungus (which is far preferable).

In hot, dry conditions, a dead body will naturally mummify instead of decomposing. The crew members of the American *Lady Be Good* military plane were found mummified 17 years after they crashed in the Libyan desert.

An emu has an inflatable neck sac that it uses to make strange noises – a bit like the funny sounds you can make when you let down a balloon.

Clarence Dally was an American researcher who worked on early X-rays. His habit of testing X-ray tubes on his own hands caused cancers so aggressive that his arms had to be amputated.

*Oophagy* is the eating of eggs in the womb by developing shark embryos. That's taking sibling rivalry a step too far!

Marine bloodworms have such pale skin that you can see their blood flowing underneath it.

After problems on re-entry, the crew of the Russian *Voskhod 2* spacecraft landed in the middle of the Ural Mountains. They spent a whole night surrounded by howling wolves before they were rescued.

Dogs will quite happily eat their own vomit.

Shark liver oil may sound foul, but it's bursting with vitamins and healing substances. It has been used by fisherman for centuries to soothe skin complaints and wounds.

Camels are cool customers; they begin to sweat only when the temperature goes above 41 degrees Celsius (106 degrees Fahrenheit). This saves them about five litres of water a day.

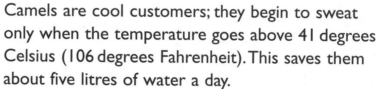

*Mal de Débarquement Syndrome* is seasickness without the sea. After being on a boat, sufferers still feel like they are in rough seas when they are back on land. Some can feel queasy for years afterwards.

The *Cobra Lily* plant looks like a rearing cobra, complete with leaves that resemble forked tongues. It has a gooey secretion and downward pointing hairs on its leaves to drag unsuspecting insects inside for food.

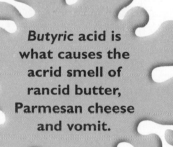

*Butyric* acid is what causes the acrid smell of rancid butter, Parmesan cheese and vomit.

If you use a sponge in the bath or shower, then you should think twice – it harbours more bacteria than the toilet bowl!

If you can face cooking pongy *stinkhorn* mushrooms, they taste of fish.

While on a plant-hunting expedition in Hawaii, 19th-century Scottish botanist David Douglas fell into a pit trap. A bull then fell on top of him and killed him.

If ground temperatures are cold enough during a storm, rain can turn into ice as it falls. During the North American ice storm of 1998, many barns collapsed from the weight of the ice on their roofs, crushing the animals inside.

Most types of tarantula will eat each other, so if you're thinking of having one as a pet, don't get another one to keep it company.

The tongue of a blue whale is the size of an elephant.

Jellyfish have no bones, no cartilage, no heart, no blood, no eyes and no brain. But they can sting you!

Tar pits are natural tar pools that have been around for thousands of years. Because they're so old, they're full of the fossilized remains of animals that have come to a sticky end in there.

*Trypanophobia* is the fear of medical procedures involving injections or hypodermic needles and affects around 10 per cent of American adults.

The mother of all acnes is known as *acne fulminans*, meaning 'exploding eruptions'.

The giant squid's body contains high levels of ammonium chloride, so it tastes horrid to humans. Sperm whales love it, though.

The pretty foxglove is also known as 'dead man's bells' and 'witches' gloves' as it is highly toxic, causing symptoms such as vomiting, delirium, convulsions and heart attacks.

The teeth of sharks are constantly being replaced. One shark can get through 30,000 teeth in its lifetime.

Without the pull of normal gravity, body fluids move to the upper body. This means that astronauts in space have bulging neck veins, a swollen face and lots of nasal mucus.

Pigs will eat any kind of faeces – their own, another animal's, human – they're not fussy!

The roots of the American *bloodroot* plant contain a toxic blood-red sap that causes lesions on the skin.

Scottish biologist Alexander Fleming was so messy that his laboratory was often littered with mouldy old dishes – that's how he discovered the antibiotic *penicillin*.

Monkeypox is a mild form of smallpox, which covers the victim in blisters and pustules. It's still much worse than chickenpox, though.

Salt stops the growth of bacteria and fungi, so was sometimes used to preserve dead bodies.

Deadly hydrogen cyanide gas smells of almonds... but 40 per cent of people cannot smell it.

**Four square kilometres (about 2 and a half square miles) of land can contain up to a million worms.**

Antiseptics killed more soldiers than diseases did during the First World War. They would destroy the body's natural defences and allow bacteria inside deep wounds to take over.

**Doctors have been used as torturers throughout history. They know exactly where it hurts!**

Viruses were purposely introduced in Australia to reduce the rabbit population. *Myxomatosis* gave the poor bunnies fatal tumours and *rabbit calicivirus* made them bleed to death.

Water and electricity are a deadly combination, as water conducts electricity. No one told poor Claude François, who was electrocuted when he tried to fix a light fitting whilst standing in a filled bath.

Bacteria have been around for billions of years. If some are wiped out by an enemy such as drugs, the rest will mutate and become resistant. We can never win the battle…

Some sea spiders have six pairs of legs. That's some creepy-crawly.

**Male elephants go through phases of madness. They become very aggressive and a tar-like substance is secreted from glands at the side of the head.**

**Ball lightning is the scariest form of lightning. A deadly ball of electricity hovers eerily in the air like a little spaceship, ready to strike.**

*Spider angiomas* are harmless bumps on the surface of the skin. Made up of small blood vessels, they have a red spot in the middle with branches leading off, like a red spider's web.

The superbug **MRSA** can affect healthy people and kill them within four days. Don't think you can escape it in hospital, as that's the most likely place to pick it up!

**Lying on your right side helps excess gas escape from the stomach more easily, so you can burp yourself to sleep.**

In 1971, the crew of *Soyuz 11* space shuttle died after a broken valve allowed them to be exposed to the vacuum of space. Without air, their bodies would have exploded before they suffocated.

During the Second World War, American scientists planned to release bomb-carrying bats over Japan that would hide in buildings until the tiny bombs went off. The war ended before they finished their research so they never found out if it worked.

A *parasitic twin* is a foetus without a brain or internal organs that grows inside a normally developing twin. Kazakh boy Alamjan Nematilaev was seven years old before doctors realized he had the body of his twin inside him.

*Rat-tailed maggots* are hoverfly larvae. Their 'tail' is a kind of snorkel that can be as long as 15 centimetres (6 inches) and allows the maggot to breathe through it, if submerged.

The *gastrocolic reflex* is the name for what happens when you eat and your body decides you need to make room for the food by getting rid of some at the other end!

Cows can get *lumpyskin disease* if bitten by insects carrying the infection. (The clue to the symptoms is in the name.)

Sweat bees are attracted to the salt in human sweat and some are emerald green in colour. Don't worry, the sting hurts only a little bit.

At 28,000 degrees Celsius (50,432 degrees Fahrenheit) a lightning bolt is five times hotter than the surface of the sun.

Acid rain is caused by industrial gases like sulphur dioxide. In highly industrialized areas, the pH level of acid rain can be lower than 2.4 – more acidic than vinegar.

Bats' teeth are razor sharp so that they can chomp through hard insect shells.

It's important to drink enough water, but drinking too much can be dangerous. *Water intoxication* makes the brain swell and in severe cases will stop it functioning.

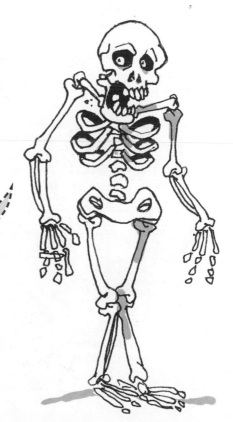

African honeybees are known as killer bees because they will swarm at the slightest provocation, entirely covering their victim.

Baboon spiders have large pads on the end of their legs that look like a baboon's feet.

Scientists have warned that our neighbouring galaxy, *Andromeda*, is heading for a collision with the *Milky Way* (our galaxy) in the distant future. If Earth is near the collision site, it will disappear in a less than a second. No one will feel a thing, though, so that's okay.

Tarantulas have eight eyes, but some species can't see a thing with them! They rely on their extreme sensitivity to vibrations and their sense of touch to catch their prey.

Ancient Greek physician Herophilos was the first to study the human body by dissecting it (opening it up). He did most of his studies on living people, but it was thought to be okay because they were only criminals.

The air pollution in Victorian London was so bad that the smelly fogs were nicknamed 'pea-soupers'.

When the liver stops working properly, the skin and the whites of the eyes turn yellow. Yellow fever got its name from these symptoms.

*Hairy wart and foot rot are infections affecting animals with hoofs.*

Russian scientist Alexander Bogdanov had many blood transfusions in the belief that they made him feel younger. In fact it was a blood transfusion that killed him, since the blood came from a student carrying malaria and tuberculosis.

Marine bloodworms grow up to 35 centimetres (about 14 inches) in length and have four jaws that are so strong they can cause agony if they bite!

The secretive Aghori tribe is so fearless of death that members live in graveyards, use human bones and ash in their rituals, and drink from human skulls.

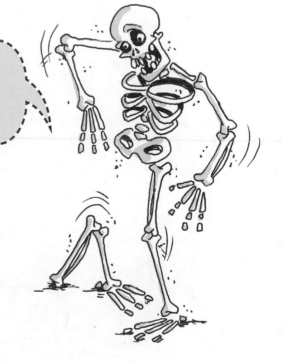

The *tarantula hawk* is a type of wasp with a stinger that is 7 millimetres (1/3 inch) long. The sting is as painful as you'd expect!

The venom of the Asian giant hornet is a nasty cocktail of chemicals: as well as a pain-causing substance, it contains an enzyme strong enough to dissolve skin and a scent to attract more hornets to the victim.

When you cut an onion, the gas released reacts with the water in your eyes to produce a diluted form of sulphuric acid.

The world's deadliest tornado hit Bangladesh in 1989. It destroyed an area of 6 square kilometres (about 2 and a half square miles) and killed 1,300 people.

*Vog* is the toxic fog containing sulphur dioxide and other nasty gases that appears after a volcano eruption. Not only does it cause breathing problems, it stinks, too.

*Hyalophagia* is the eating of glass. Only mad people and circus performers do it.

Many 18th-century milkmaids were immune to the deadly smallpox infection. English doctor Edward Jenner linked this to their getting pus on their hands from cows infected with cowpox. It may have been nasty, but it inoculated them.

An ostrich's eye is bigger than its brain. Have a look next time you see one but don't get too close – what it lacks in brains it makes up for in leg muscles.

In 1949, a monkey called Albert II became the first monkey to travel in space. Unfortunately, poor Albert died on impact when he returned from his mission.

A warning sign of an approaching tsunami is the sea receding dramatically, leaving fish flapping about on the sand. Resist the urge to have a look, just run!

Struggling in quicksand will give you that sinking feeling... the gloopy mixture contains a lot of water, so if a person relaxes they will float and be able to get out using slow movements.

Some fungal skin infections glow in the dark.

Frogs, rats, wasps, and chicken embryos, fungi, have all been sent into space to research the effects of space flight on them. They weren't all in the same rocket though!

Elephants die when their teeth are worn down and they can't feed properly. They have five sets of teeth in their lifetime, but would live longer if they had more.

The leg bones of a bat are so thin that it can't walk on them. They would snap if it tried.

The pupil of an octopus's eye is rectangular.

Heartburn is caused by stomach acid being regurgitated into the oesophagus. The acid causes a burning sensation in the chest, throat and sometimes even the jaw.

Ever wondered why you want to vomit if you see someone else do it? Scientists believe this is an evolved trait from ancient times; if one of a group foraging for food was sick, chances were they had all eaten something bad and had to get rid of it quickly.

Emu fat is a very good skin moisturiser. It won't make you run any faster, though.

Camel urine is thick and syrupy. Since camels often have to survive on little water, their kidneys are extremely efficient.

In his study on jellyfish, Dr Jack Barnes purposely stung himself and his 9-year-old son with the tiny but highly venomous *irukandji* jellyfish. All in the name of research!

Ants cannot chew their food. They have to chop away at it with their *mandibles* (jaws) that move sideways, like scissors.

The earliest transplant operation is said to have been performed in the 3rd century by twin saints Cosmas and Damian. They replaced the ulcerated leg of a patient with the healthy one of an Ethiopian. How successful it was is anybody's guess!

An explosion during an experiment left German chemist Robert Bunsen blinded in one eye by flying glass.

Lobsters and octopuses have blue blood. This is because the protein that transports oxygen round their bodies is rich in copper.

Giant tubeworms live in deep ocean seabeds and have no mouth or gut. They can be up to 3 metres (10 feet long) and live on a cocktail of chemicals spewed out of the earth that kills just about everything else.

Female dogs were used during Russian space flight experiments, as they did not need to lift their legs to urinate. No room for that in a space capsule!

18th-century Italian scientist Luigi Galvani discovered electrical impulses in nerves and muscles whilst doing experiments on static electricity. A static-loaded scalpel touched a dissected frog and its leg hopped into life!

Southern California is heading north! It is moving very slowly and will collide with Alaska in about 150 million years' time.

Sharks have no bones. Their skeletons are made of cartilage, which is lighter and more flexible.

If you fell into a black hole, you'd eventually come out again as light and bits of ash.

Bright colours on animals and insects warn predators that they taste yucky. The ladybird also secretes yellow, foul-smelling goo for any that haven't got the message!

A *pyroclastic flow* is what causes death and destruction when a volcano erupts, as in Pompeii in 79 AD. It is a boiling concoction of ash and toxic gas that travels at 150 kilometres (95 miles) per hour, demolishing everything in its path.

The Australian ghost bat looks even spookier than a regular bat. Its thin wing skin and pale fur make it look spectral at night.

A 4,000-year-old mummified man found in the Austrian Alps was found to have an arrowhead lodged in his shoulder.

Freak waves are a natural ocean phenomenon and can reach heights of 15 metres (45 feet). They are often blamed when vessels disappear suddenly without trace.

A mudflow or mudslide can travel at speeds of 80 kilometres (50 miles) an hour, trapping and suffocating everyone and everything in its path.

**CAUTION! Some of these World Record Facts are highly dangerous. They have been set by people who have trained for a long time and received strict medical guidance. Don't try any of them at home!**

The largest foreign object left in a patient was a pair of 33 centimetre (13 inch)-long forceps, sewn inside Indian woman Meena Purohit after a Caesarean birth. The implement was discovered only when she had another operation four years later!

Robert Mark Burns peeled and ate a lemon in 46.53 seconds. He was sour-faced for hours afterwards.

Australian Stuart Ross ate 15 fiery-hot jalapeño chilli peppers in one minute.

The most bloodthirsty parasite is the hookworm. Hookworms suck so much blood from the intestine that an infected person can become anaemic.

The heaviest marine crustacean is the American lobster. One caught in 1977 weighed over 20 kilograms (44 pounds). The lobster doesn't chew food in its mouth, it has teeth in its stomach to do that.

The biggest underpants in the world, bearing the slogan 'Pants to Poverty', measured 14.4 metres (47 feet 3 inches) wide. Let's hope they were clean ones.

American Lee Redmond's hideously long, curved nails have a total length of 7.51 metres (24 feet 7 inches). How does she go to the bathroom? Carefully!

An Arctic-dwelling whale known as a *narwhal* has a single enormous tusk. The tusk can grow to a length of 3 metres (9 feet 10 inches), which makes it the longest whale tooth.

The world's hairiest man is Yu Zhenhuan from China – his body is 96 per cent covered in long hair!

The elephant seal has a kind of trunk that it uses to make scary roaring noises. It can hold its breath for more than 80 minutes, longer than any other non-ocean-dwelling mammal.

The largest venom glands are over a centimetre (half an inch) long and are found in the Brazilian wandering spider. The venom inside is one of the most deadly, too.

British man Gordon Mattinson can make his face look so gruesome that he has won the World Gurning Championships 10 times.

'Snakeman' Jackie Bibby held eight big rattlesnakes in his mouth for 12.5 seconds. He's so snake-mad that he got married in a snake pit!

The highest number of cows killed by lightning was 68 Jerseys that were sheltering under a tree, struck during a storm in Australia.

Female *Queen Alexandra's birdwing* butterflies from Papua New Guinea are the biggest in the world and can have a wingspan of 30 centimetres (12 inches). Locals use blowguns to kill the rare butterflies so they can sell them to collectors.

The North Pacific Gyre is a huge vortex of slow, clockwise-revolving ocean water. It has drawn so much litter and waste into its centre that it is the largest ocean landfill site. It's known as The Great Pacific Garbage Patch!

Before sensible boxing rules were introduced, Jack Jones and Patsy Tunney beat each other to a pulp in a fight that had 276 rounds and lasted 4 hours 30 minutes.

The water in the largest hot spring in Deildartunguhver, Iceland, is close to boiling point – so unless you want to make human soup, stay away!

A British man survived 90 per cent burns after an exploding canister covered him in petrol while he was filling his moped in 1996.

The largest parasite of all is the tapeworm, that can even get in to human intestines. Some live for up to 20 years and the biggest known was 18 metres (60 feet) long.

Desert locusts have been the most destructive insects on the planet for thousands of years. A day's food for a regular swarm of 50 million locusts would feed 500 people for a whole year.

The first hairy earwig sanctuary was created in the 1960s in Sarawak, northern Borneo.

American Benjamin Drucker had 745 surgical needles stuck into his body in 2 hours 21 minutes to become the world record holder for the most piercings with 18-gauge surgical needles.

With his swollen gums, missing teeth, bald patches and overgrown claws, Chi-Chi the African sand dog has won the World's Ugliest Dog Contest seven times.

The most dangerous sea urchin is the *flower sea urchin*. Brushing against its toxic spines will cause severe pain, breathing problems and paralysis.

The *Ongaonga tree nettle* in New Zealand has the most dangerous plant sting. Brushing against it causes a sting that lasts for days. Falling into it can be fatal.

Sandeep Kaur's face and scalp were ripped off in one piece when her pigtails got caught in a threshing machine as a child. She had the first ever full-face transplant operation and went on to become a nurse.

The Black Sea is the largest *meromictic basin*. This means that it has deadly hydrogen sulphide gas trapped in its depths that could be released if there were an earthquake.

American stuntman Ted Batchelor's body was on fire for 2 minutes 36 seconds during a fire stunt in 2004, making it the longest full-body burn.

African Johannes Relleke was attacked by bees in 1962 and had the most number of bee stings ever removed: 2,443!

Indian man Radhakant Bajpai has the longest ear hair in the world, measuring 13.2 centimetres (5.19 inches). He believes it's a gift from God.

The largest toxic cloud, containing cancer-causing *beryllium*, covered an area of 300 kilometres (186 miles) and came from a 1990 factory fire in Kazakhstan.

**Australian Grant Denyer was kissed by 62 people in one minute. That's 62 lots of bacteria-ridden saliva!**

The world's most used method of execution is death by firing squad.

**When is a worm not a worm? When it's the world's smallest snake, the *thread snake*. It looks like a worm, but if you look closely you can see its snaky eyes. It won't see you, as it's blind!**

Ian Sharman ran the London marathon in 2007… dressed as Elvis! He broke the world record for the fastest man to run as Elvis, finishing in 2 hours and 57 minutes.

The largest animals to be gobbled up by big, carnivorous *pitcher plants* are rats, frogs and lizards.

The *thresher shark* has the longest fin, with its tail fin being as long as the body and head. It's also known as a *swiveltail*, since it uses the huge fin to whack its prey unconscious before devouring it.

Carbon dioxide-filled Lake Nyos in West Africa is the world's deadliest lake. Sudden eruptions release the gas without warning, suffocating animals and people nearby.

**Human extinguisher Antti Karvinen put out 36 fire torches with his mouth in one minute in 2000.**

The record for sharing a coffin with the most cockroaches is held by 'Jungle' John LaMedica. He lay in a transparent coffin and had 20,050 giant Madagascan hissing cockroaches poured on top of him!

The great white shark is the largest predatory fish and can be as long as 6 metres (20 feet). Humans are generally too bony for it to eat, but it will still take a bite!

The world's most pierced man, Luis Antonio Agüero, has more than 175 ring piercings in his face alone. He has 55 more piercings in other parts of his body!

The ferocious *wolverine* is the largest land-dwelling weasel. It's also known as the *skunk bear*, as it will give off a nasty smell if annoyed.

The floppy nose of an old male *proboscis* monkey can be as long as 17.5 centimetres (7 inches) and hangs over its mouth.

The hairiest frog is… the hairy frog! The male adult frogs develop hairy thighs during the breeding season.

The Venus flytrap plant can snap its leaves shut around a juicy insect in just one tenth of a second.

American Cathie Jung has deformed her body in the way Victorians used to. She has the narrowest corseted waist measurement of just 38 centimetres (15 inches).

British performer Scott Bell didn't get cold feet for his record attempt. He walked 76.2 metres (250 feet) over burning hot embers.

The fish with the most eyes is the six-eyed *Pacific spookfish*.

The worst firework disaster killed around 800 people in Paris during royal wedding celebrations in 1770. Firework sparks ignited other fireworks prematurely, starting a fire and causing the crowds to stampede.

At 32 centimetres (13 inches) tall, the African goliath frog is the largest frog on earth. It can jump 3 metres (10 feet) in one go, but can only do this a couple of times before it needs a rest.

The ocean sunfish is the heaviest bony fish and can weigh up to 2 tonnes (4,400 pounds). It looks like the ugliest, too – it has one bulging eye, it can't close its mouth and its toxic, sandpapery skin is covered in mucus.

The vicious honey badger is the most fearless mammal: it can kill and eat a snake measuring 150 centimetres (5 feet) in 15 minutes and can take hundreds of bee stings too!

Palaeontologists discovered the stalest vomit ever in Peterborough, England, in 2002: 160 million-year-old fossilized vomit from a marine reptile.

The largest fish egg ever discovered was that of a whale shark in 1953. It was more than 30 centimetres (1 foot) long and had a live embryo wriggling around inside it!

The heart of a blue whale is the largest of any animal. The aorta is 23 centimetres (9 inches) wide and the heart itself is the size of a small car. Plenty of room for a family of four.

The World Ball Cup is a testicle-cooking competition held annually in Serbia. Teams of chefs cook bull, boar and camel testicles.

A *haggis* is a sheep's stomach stuffed with a tasty filling of heart, liver and lungs. The furthest distance a haggis has been thrown is 55.11 metres (180 feet 10 inches).

Louise Hollis has been growing her toenails since 1982 and the combined length of all ten nails is over 2 metres (over 7 feet). She may not be able to wear shoes or walk properly, but at least she's a world record holder!

Park ranger Roy C Sullivan survived being struck by lightning. Not once, not twice, but seven times.

The largest feline carnivore, the Siberian tiger, can munch 45 kilograms (100 pounds) of meat in one go. It can eat a bear but luckily it isn't too interested in munching on people.

Attention-seeker Jerome Abramovitch inflates his forehead and cheeks by injecting saline into them, creating a disfigured 'Elephant Man' look.

Canadian ginger tabby cat Jake has 28 toes – 7 on each paw!

At the World Mosquito Killing Championships in 1995, Henri Pellonpaa killed 21 mosquitoes in 5 minutes... using just his hand!

People desperate for tickets to see the 2006 Filipino game show *Wowowee* stampeded, causing the most game show deaths (74 people were trampled to death).

*Bombay blood* (h-h) is such a rare blood group that anyone needing an urgent blood transfusion of that type would not be able to get it, and would most likely die.

Russian dog Laika was the first dog to enter Earth's orbit, but she was not meant to return. Her food for the tenth day contained fatal poison, but faulty temperature controls meant that she died from heat exhaustion a few hours after take-off anyway.

The largest garlic festival in Gilroy, California, lasts three days. Garlic ice cream, anyone?

13,000-year-old skeletons discovered in caves in Indonesia were found to be from a race of little people that were just a metre (3 feet 3 inches) tall.

The most toxic man-made chemical, known as TCDD, is 150,000 times more deadly than cyanide. Just what the world needs!

Monster saltwater crocodiles killed 9,980 Japanese soldiers who tried to cross Burmese mangrove swamps in 1945, making it the worst crocodile attack ever.

The slime eel is the only fish that can sneeze. It burrows into other fish, whether they're dead or not, and eats their internal organs. Then it produces extra slime to slither out again and sneezes any excess away!

The deadliest natural toxin doesn't come from any plant or animal but from bad food. *Clostridium botulinum* is more poisonous than arsenic or snake venom and causes the deadly illness *botulism*.

Australian Andrew Hajinikitas drank 120 millilitres (4.2 fluid ounces) of tongue-obliterating Tabasco Sauce in 30 seconds.

The most expensive food is black, smelly fish eggs: Almas caviar is worth £20,000 ($36,000) per kilogram.

The worst lightning strike disaster killed 81 people when a Boeing 707 jet was struck in 1963.

Croatian police seized 10 mobile phones in 2000. The phones were cleverly disguised pistols that could fire deadly bullets if the number 5678 was dialled.

The most expensive bar of soap contains fat from former Italian Prime Minister Silvio Berlusconi and costs £10,000 ($18,000).

Argentinians eat the most beef – they get through over 2 million tonnes (4 billion pounds) a year!

American Rob Williams made a ham, cheese and lettuce sandwich using his feet in 1 minute 57 seconds.

The world's oldest piece of cake was found in an Ancient Egyptian tomb and is 4,200 years old!

The biggest Japanese spider crab ever found had a leg span of 3.69 metres (12 feet 1 inches). These monsters can live for 100 years.

The largest rodent is the South American *capybara*, which looks like a gigantic guinea pig. Capybaras in Brazil were found to be carriers of the severe bacterial infection *Rocky Mountain spotted fever*.

Canadian Aaron Gregg juggled three running chainsaws and made 86 catches. Some people would give their right arm to do that!

Irishman Vincent Pilkington killed and plucked 100 turkeys in 7 hours and 32 minutes in 1978.

Canadian Christopher Tyler Ing had a nipple hair that was 8.89 centimetres (3.5 inches) long.

The liver is the largest internal organ and can be up to 22 centimetres (8.6 inches) long. If it's not working properly, just one of the things that can happen is that your fingernails drop off.

The Peregrine falcon is the fastest creature on earth. It can knock out a smaller bird with a single blow and will break the bird's neck if it hasn't died on impact. Then the falcon will use its sharp beak and talons to rip the prey apart and eat it!

The most polluted town is Dzerzhinsk in Russia, where life expectancy for a man is 42 years old. The town is full of factories producing chlorine, pesticides and chemical weapons.

Large, biting *tsetse flies* are the least picky bloodsuckers of vertebrates. They'll bite anything that has a backbone – they're not fussy!

The largest insect swarm ever was made up of 10 billion locusts that invaded Kenya in 1954.

Male African cicadas produce the loudest insect sound. By vibrating their special membranes, their call can reach 106 decibels!

The longest millipede ever discovered was 38.7 centimetres (15.2 inches) long and had 256 legs!

Japanese *macaques* are the northernmost population of non-human primates. Their faces, hands and bottoms are bright red!

The largest burrowing animal is the Australian wombat. Small wombats may look cute, but a fully-grown one can charge at a man, knock him over and leave a 2 centimetre (1 inch) deep bite in his leg!

Anaconda snakes have the biggest difference between the sexes amongst vertebrates: the females are five times bigger than the males.

The largest land carnivore is the polar bear, which spends the whole winter feasting on seals. It can also manage a huge walrus and even a beluga whale.

**Indian boy Devendra Harne has 12 fingers and 13 toes.**

The most expensive soup is made with shark's fin, sea cucumbers and other yucky (and illegal) stuff. *Buddha-jumps-over-the-wall* soup costs £108 and has to be ordered five days in advance.

The brain removed from an American man in 1992 weighed 2.3 kilograms (5 pounds 1 ounce); almost twice as much as an average one. He had more brains than most!

The largest spider is the goliath bird-eating spider, which can have a leg span of up to 30 centimetres (12 inches). That would cover your school ruler!

Alan 'Nasty' Nash crushed 23 eggs with his toes in 30 seconds. Cheese omelette, anyone?

The USA has the largest death row population in the world, with more than 3,000 prisoners awaiting execution.

The longest stick insects are found in the rainforests of Borneo and can have a total length of more than 54 centimetres (20 inches). They're so gangly, they often have legs missing that have got ripped off during skin shedding.

The largest cat is a *liger* – a lion mates with a tigress and the hybrid offspring grows up to be twice as big. Imagine if you grew up to be twice as tall as your dad!

The deadliest magic trick is the bullet-catching trick – at least 11 people have died whilst performing it.

The parasite that affects the most humans is also the most fertile – a female roundworm can produce 26 million eggs in her lifetime. She must die of exhaustion!

The gaboon viper has the longest fangs of any snake. It delivers a venom so toxic that the affected body part often has to be amputated.

*Nepenthes albomarginata* is the fussiest insect-eating plant – it will only eat termites! A hungry plant will lure 22 termites a minute into its tubular leaves.

'Rubber boy' Daniel Browning Smith can dislocate his arms and legs to squeeze through a tennis racket- sized hole in 15 seconds!

Peter Dowdeswell ate 4.5 kilograms (12 pounds) of ice cream in 45.5 seconds. Then he had the mother of all brain freezes.

Bert is the reserve Deputy Sheriff for the Los Angeles County Sheriff's Department. He might kick you if you break the law, but that's because he's a camel.

The lava that comes from the Ol Doinyo Lengai volcano in Tanzania is the coldest in the world... but it's still 600 degrees Celsius (1,112 degrees Fahrenheit).

The furthest distance a cowpat has been tossed is 81.1 metres (226 feet). Best to stand well clear at that event!

After having her nose, lips and chin chewed off by her pet dog, Isabelle Dinoire received the first ever partial face transplant. In the operation, new parts from a recently deceased body were attached to her face.

American Cecil Walker gulped eight sausages in one minute by swallowing them whole!

Gallstones can form in the gallbladder and make a person ill. The largest one ever removed weighed 6.29 kilograms (almost 14 pounds). That's as heavy as two babies!

An armadillo has huge claws that can be 20 centimetres (8 inches) long. It also has up to 100 teeth.

New Zealander Lucky Diamond Rich is tattooed on every inch of his body – even his gums.

# Gruesome
# Random Facts

A coffin, false limbs and dead bats were among items handed in to Transport for London's lost property office in 2006.

An 'inexperienced traveller' sent her month-old grandson through the hand luggage x-ray machine at Los Angeles airport. The baby was rushed to hospital but fortunately had not received a dangerous dose of radiation.

A pair of pongy socks left in a car by rock singer Bryan Adams raised over £500 ($900) for charity!

A body will decompose in water four times more quickly than on land.

US taxidermist Jeanette Hall can give you an everlasting memento of your pet – a cushion made from its fur!

Pretty garden flowers such as buttercups, daffodils, lupins and sweet peas are all poisonous if eaten, causing stomach cramps and vomiting.

Some birds will place ants in their own feathers. The ants then spray formic acid and kill any parasites.

On 19 March 2006, Benjamin Franklin was electrocuted and died after flying his kite in a storm – he'd lengthened the short string with some copper wire. Would you believe he was actually an electrician?

Escape artist Joe Burras tried the 'buried alive' trick in 1990, but it ended up not being an illusion; he was crushed to death by the cement poured on top of the box he was in.

One Seattle tourist attraction is the Gum Wall – a brick wall covered with old chewing gum in every colour imaginable.

Every decade, one million people die in violent natural disasters like earthquakes and hurricanes. This figure could be set to rise.

A hippopotamus can run faster than a man (and then squash him)!

Entertainer Roy Horn was seriously injured in 2003 when a tiger he used in his act picked him up in its mouth and ran off with him. He suffered severe blood loss and brain swelling.

A thief who snatched a bulging bag from a doorstep in Scotland was probably disappointed with his smelly loot: 60 dirty nappies, put out for a nappy laundering service.

The female black widow spider can devour up to 20 males in one day.

The remains of Mahatma Gandhi are floating in several of the world's major rivers. He had asked that his ashes be scattered in them.

**Bear-gardens** were 16th-century arenas where hunting dogs would be set upon a bear and replaced as they were killed or wounded. That was entertainment in those days!

Sally Orange from Nottingham, England, ran the London marathon in 2007 in 4 hours and 8 minutes. She broke the world record for the fastest woman dressed as a superhero!

*Dracula ants* are so called because they chew holes in and suck the blood of their own larvae.

A German man dropped a kitchen knife on his foot, chopping off a toe. As he hopped around calling an ambulance and trying to stop the bleeding, his cat ran off with the toe and it was never seen again.

The electric chair was invented by a dentist, who was inspired after seeing a man get electrocuted. Let's hope he didn't try it out on his patients!

A Serbian man was given permission to bury his mother in his back garden when she died ten years ago. Since then, dozens more dead friends and relatives have been buried there.

It's believed that elongated skulls found in Mexico were created by binding babies' heads to deform the skull as it developed.

The skin of a hippopotamus is so thick that even a bullet cannot penetrate it.

An 8-year-old girl thought to have been eaten by wild animals in Vietnam returned 18 years later. She had been living in the jungle the whole time and had become feral – she couldn't speak, her hair was down to her legs and her body was blackened.

An American woman had her dead husband's diamond cufflinks made into a stickpin… that she wore in a piercing on her throat.

Humans are the only species that drinks the breast milk of other animals.

An Indian man accidentally swallowed a toothbrush…and then waited a week before seeing a doctor. He only acted when the stomach pains became unbearable.

Three Moscow men demanded substantial compensation when they found a dead rat in their packet of spicy croutons. The rat was spiced too, but they didn't fancy it.

Venezuelan scientist Dr Jesús Rivas wades through leech-infested waters to find huge anaconda snakes! He has found over 900, which he has measured and taken blood samples from for his research.

The average cremated person's ashes weigh 4 kilograms (9 pounds).

Danish artist Marco Evaristti invited some close friends for dinner and served them pasta with meatballs that contained his own liposuction fat.

A canoeist who stopped to help a fisherman pull a fish from an African river ended up needing 50 stitches in his arm – the fish was a whopping Zambezi shark.

US World Cup lacrosse player Diane Whipple was killed outside her apartment by her neighbours' two huge mastiff dogs. She bled to death from throat wounds.

A man received compensation after he took what he thought was a handful of peanuts in a restaurant, tipped them into his mouth, and crunched on a cockroach.

American playwright Tennessee Williams choked to death on a bottle top.

An Austrian hunter managed to shoot himself as he was shaking the snow out of his rifle.

A 9-year-old girl from an Indian tribe was married to a stray dog in a ceremony intended to ward off an evil omen.

A Belgian man set his house on fire and suffered burns when he tried to cremate his pet dog's body at home.

Irritating tarantula hairs have been used in the past to make joke itching powders.

Pub owners in Southampton, England, checked their CCTV when a urinal went missing. It showed a man removing the urinal and taking it away in a rucksack.

A Swiss man came home from his holidays to find a dead body on his settee! It was not known how or why the person had got into his house.

**Early advertisements for coffee claimed it was a cure for scurvy and gout.**

The bodies of a dead couple who were frozen in the hope that future medical science could bring them back to life had to be cremated when the freezer broke down.

A Brisbane café owner was fined after the discovery of a rat on his premises. The rat was dead and stuck to the floor after being painted over rather than removed!

A Hong Kong man has kept a sheet of skin peeled from his sunburnt chest in 1979, in the hope that it will set a world record. He also says that the 21.6 centimetre (8.5 inch) piece of skin is in the shape of China!

**70 per cent of our DNA is the same as that of a slug.**

Plastic surgeon Dr Robert Ersek performed liposuction on himself... on live television.

Police raided a warehouse in Peru and set free 4,000 frogs that were destined to be a juice made from liquidized frogs!

At least 186 people have died trying to climb Mount Everest. Most corpses are left behind, due to difficulties in bringing them down.

Airport officials at Logan Airport, Boston, stopped a passenger taking the severed head of a seal on to a plane. The man claimed to be a biology professor who wanted the head for research.

**Between 1902 and 1907, one tiger killed 436 people in India.**

Octopuses can squeeze through small cracks – some have been known to escape from their tanks to have a slither around outside!

**A German inventor has discovered a way of making dead cats into diesel fuel. One dead cat can make 2.5 litres of fuel.**

A Dutch woman who was visiting a cemetery fell on top of a coffin when an old grave collapsed and she tumbled in.

An Australian diver was saved by his lead-weight vest when a shark tried to swallow him head first! He escaped with a broken nose and bite marks on his chest and back.

500 people paid to watch the first public autopsy in 170 years. Professor Gunther von Hagens sliced and sawed the body of a 72-year-old man and removed its internal organs for his fascinated audience.

An Italian toy manufacturer caused outrage when it brought out a range of toy atomic bombs.

A crocodile cannot stick its tongue out.

Artist Gabriela Rivera covered herself in raw meat for one of her exhibitions.

Chinese 'Snake Man' Liu Lang can stick a snake through his nostril and bring it out through his mouth!

Staff at an acupuncture clinic locked up and went home… forgetting about a woman in a treatment room. The woman had to remove the needles herself and call for help.

Dogs bite a million Americans every year. That's an awful lot of bites!

When New Age healer Jack Temple died in 2004, he left toenail clippings and hair samples from famous clients such as Jerry Hall and Cherie Blair.

Passengers on a Saudi Airlines flight were startled when a rat escaped from a large rucksack… followed by 79 more!

Lasers, sandpaper, acids and toxins are all used in modern cosmetic surgery. It can't be worth it, surely?

During the festival of San Fermín in the Spanish city of Pamplona, people volunteer to be chased through the streets by fighting bulls. Some have been gored and trampled, but it doesn't put thrill-seekers off!

**Actress Peg Entwistle killed herself by jumping off the giant letter H in the Hollywood sign.**

A Dutch surgeon was disciplined after taking home bits of human flesh for his wife to use in the training of rescue dogs.

**Peruvian hairless dogs may not get fleas, but they often have blackheads and acne!**

Sword-swallower Hannibal Helmurto was taken to hospital after cutting his throat with one of his swords during a show, making an audience member faint in horror!

Californian authorities were puzzled by the corpse of a wet-suited diver in the middle of a forest that had burnt down. It emerged that helicopters used giant buckets of seawater to put out the fire, so the diver must have been scooped up with the water!

Olympic skier Ross Milne died after skiing into a tree during a practice session in 1964.

Students attending a summer criminology course in Florida were startled to find a real dead body at a fake crime scene! The man had died of natural causes.

**A polar bear in a US zoo had its rotten tooth removed using a hammer and chisel.**

**A woman was warned to keep her ferocious cat under control after it repeatedly attacked her postman!**

An Australian whose toilet was blocked found that the cause was a python measuring 2.1 metres (7 feet) in the septic tank.

A whale from the North Atlantic got so lost that it swam into London and died of starvation – there are no deepwater squid in the Thames! Its skeleton later went on display in the city, measuring 4.8 metres (16 feet).

Slovenian swimmer Martin Strel needed buckets of blood to swim across the Amazon! The blood was to be used as a distraction for flesh-eating fish and reptiles.

A blood-sucking midge beats its wings 1,046 times a second. That makes it the world record holder for the fastest muscles.

Botox injections, used to make skin less wrinkly, contain diluted *clostridium botulinum*: the deadliest natural toxin on the planet, remember?

Japanese people who cannot afford to buy graves for their deceased loved ones can instead have their ashes made into a pyramid-shaped mantelpiece ornament.

A well-meaning Russian woman decided to clean out her son's fish tank, not realising it was full of piranhas. The fish attacked her when she put her hand in to catch them and left her with serious injuries.

A Welsh man ended up in hospital after trying to staple his hand to a coffee table... for fun!

Men are six times more likely to be struck by lightning than women.

A hunter's wife opened her fridge and was startled by a duck moving inside it... as the duck had supposedly been shot dead two days earlier.

Bulldogs were bred in the 16th century for the blood sport of bull baiting: they would be set on a bull and attach themselves to its snout.

A 'urine police' force was created in Berlin in 2003 to stop people urinating on the city's historic buildings and monuments, already damaged by acidic human urine.

A US manufacturer has invented underwear with a built-in fart filter!

The *hirudo* leech has three jaws with 100 teeth in each jaw!

Mouldy training shoes left on a British train were so whiffy that they sparked a full-scale security alert in which the train was evacuated and searched.

Rattlesnakes will gather in groups to sleep, sometimes a thousand at a time.

An Australian tiger shark regurgitated an arm in 1935 and an unusual tattoo on it helped police to identify the dead person.

'Grizzly Man' Timothy Treadwell was a bear enthusiast who was killed and partially eaten by a grizzly bear in 2003. He loved bears a bit too much and had set up a tent near a salmon stream, not bothering to take anything to defend himself with!

**85 per cent of all life on Earth is plankton.**

A Croatian gardener bought a sack of soil from a building site and tipped a skeleton on to his flowerbed! The remains were of a Nazi soldier, complete with identification plates.

A Florida grandmother was bitten on the leg by an alligator in her garden. She scared it off by whacking it with her hosepipe nozzle – go for it, Grandma!

A Turkish man hid his mother's dead body in the basement and used her clothes to disguise himself so he could collect her pension.

Men and women pierce their cheeks in ceremonies held during the Phuket Vegetarian Festival. One man has had a crossbar inserted through his cheek, with the bicycle still attached!

100 lightning bolts strike the Earth every second, frazzling anything (and anyone) in their path.

Writer William Burroughs killed his wife when he tried to shoot a glass off the top of her head.

A Kansas student was charged with battery when it was alleged he purposely vomited on his teacher. The student's father insisted that the chuck-up was due to exam stress.

There are 6,500 species of fly in Britain and 16,000 in North America. Some suck blood, some vomit on your food, others feed on faeces – they're all pretty disgusting.

Stamps that went on sale in China to celebrate the Year of the Pig were sweet and sour pork flavoured.

**A toad will eat 10,000 insects in one summer.**

A Russian village had to be evacuated when it was hit by a plague of flies. The swarms had come from a nearby mountain of chicken manure.

A Scottish man was imprisoned for alarming neighbours by howling like a werewolf for hours on end.

A survey into music at European funerals showed that while Spaniards and Italians prefer to be seen off to the sound of classical music, Britons pick pop and Germans choose heavy metal.

A ski instructor had to be treated for shock and hypothermia after being buried in an avalanche... whilst warning his group about the dangers of avalanches!

An Israeli health spa has a special massage on offer – six lively snakes are placed on the customer's back to ease away aches and pains.

A two-faced cow was born in the US. It had three sets of teeth, two lower jaws, two tongues, two noses and a single eye socket with two eyes in it. Apart from that it was fine!

An Iranian woman's grounds for divorce were that her husband had not washed for over a year.

A Dutch art gallery displayed photographs taken from police forensics' archives. People flocked to see pictures of blood-spattered crime scenes and body bits!

Prince Henrik of Denmark upset animal lovers when he said he liked dogs...sliced and fried! He added that dog meat 'tastes like veal'.

A dog needed treatment after he ate his owner's knickers and they blocked his intestines.

Belgian gravediggers caused uproar when they held a barbecue party in the cemetery where they worked. They were cooking regular sausages, though, not body bits!

The average human body contains enough carbon to make 900 pencils.

A German wheelchair-bound hospital patient was found severely dehydrated after being stuck in a broken lift for three days and surviving on biscuits from his pocket.

South Korean man Lee Seung Seup died of exhaustion and dehydration after playing on a computer game for 50 hours without a break.

Plastic rubbish kills 100,000 marine animals every year.

A Romanian woman received a package in the post and was horrified to find it contained her father's skeleton! The graveyard he had been buried in was sold for development and the bodies returned to their relatives.

*Darwin's frog* tadpoles are swallowed by their father! They develop in his vocal sac and hop out when they're ready.

A British firm has produced novelty coffins in shapes such as a skip and a guitar!

An Austrian woman who discharged herself from hospital went home to find her family planning her funeral! They had been told in a hospital mix-up that she had died.

Incidents of food poisoning increase by 1 per cent with each 1 degree Celsius (33.8 degrees Fahrenheit) rise in weather temperature.

Whilst showing off to friends by hand-feeding sausages to his pet alligator, a Russian man was badly bitten and needed hospital treatment.

A US family was covered with urine, faeces and toilet paper when a passing coach emptied its toilet contents on to their sunroof!

A Dutch branch of McDonald's had to remove its red, mouth-shaped urinals after complaints.

Urine from male cape water buffaloes is so flammable that some tribes use it for lantern fuel.

*Vegetable caterpillars* are caterpillars with fungus growing out of them and are a Chinese delicacy.

Chilean artists Carmen Ariztia and Francisca Aninat created an exhibition that included crosses made from human bones and teeth!

## Your 1001st Gruesome Fact !

..................................................................
..................................................................
..................................................................
..................................................................
..................................................................
..................................................................
..................................................................
..................................................................

**I, the undersigned, hereby confirm that this fact is even more gruesome than stuff about blue pus and fried tarantulas.**

**Signed:** ...................................

**Date:** ...................................